THIS GREEN HOUSE

THIS GREEN HOUSE

HOME IMPROVEMENTS FOR THE ECO-SMART, THE THRIFTY, AND THE DO-IT-YOURSELFER

Joshua Piven

Illustrations by Owen Sherwood

STEWART, TABORI & CHANG | NEW YORK

Published in 2009 by Stewart, Tabori & Chang
An imprint of Harry N. Abrams, Inc.

Text copyright © 2009 Joshua L. Piven
Illustrations copyright © 2009 Owen Sherwood

Library of Congress Cataloging-in-Publication Data
Piven, Joshua.
  This green house / Joshua Piven.
      p. cm.
  ISBN 978-1-58479-786-9
  1. Energy conservation. 2. Sustainable living. 3. Green products. I.
Title.
  TJ163.3.P58 2009
  643—dc22
                    2008037828

Editor: Ann Stratton
Designer: Alissa Faden
Production Manager: Tina Cameron

The text of this book was composed in Thesis.

Stewart, Tabori & Chang books are available at special discounts when purchased
in quantity for premiums and promotions as well as fundraising or educational
use. Special editions can also be created to specification. For details, contact
specialmarkets@hnabooks.com or the address below.

Printed and bound in China
10 9 8 7 6 5 4 3 2 1

HNA
harry n. abrams, inc.
a subsidiary of La Martinière Groupe

115 West 18th Street
New York, NY 10011
www.hnabooks.com

FOR MY CHILDREN.
AND FOR YOURS.

Contents

Save the Planet One Home Improvement at a Time

Eating: Wastes land, water, and energy; creates emissions; is bad for the planet.

Working: Requires a computer; wastes energy derived from fossil fuels; creates emissions; is bad for the planet.

Sleeping: A house wastes energy derived from fossil fuels; creates emissions; is bad for the planet.

Driving: Wastes fuel; is based on extractive energy; creates emissions; is bad for the planet.

Vacation: Wastes everything. Forget it.

These days, it seems as if modern life is little more than a death sentence for the planet. You can't really do anything without somebody somewhere saying that whatever you do, you could be doing it greener. Is it any wonder, then, that recent studies indicate people are becoming so overwhelmed by "green noise" that they suffer from analysis paralysis? That they're confused, afraid to make any eco-conscious decision at all, lest it be the wrong one? Or that they really could be—should be—doing more? Or that the greenest choice they make is actually the opposite of the choice they should have made?

Here's a real-world example of this phenomenon. "Eat local" has become a mantra of the environmental movement. Reducing global shipping, the logic goes, is good for the planet because it reduces fuel consumption and, thus, emissions, pollution, and global warming. Some grocery store chains are even beginning to include "carbon labels" on their products, indicating the precise (or near-precise) quantities of energy that have gone into producing and delivering each item. Sounds good, right?

The problem is that the earth's climate varies, and not all areas are suitable for growing all things or raising all types of animals. In this context, eating local doesn't always make sense. For example, studies have calculated that the amount of fossil-fuel-derived energy needed—and the amount of pollution produced—to grow, say, hothouse tomatoes in overcast Britain may actually be greater than the amount of energy used to grow tomatoes in sunny West Africa and then ship them to the United Kingdom. So if you choose locally grown tomatoes in London, there's no net environmental savings.

As this example shows, global warming is a complex issue, and it doesn't help that the media are constantly trumpeting eco-warnings about this or that activity. *Don't flush the toilet on an airplane; it uses a quarter gallon of fuel. Don't take that free grocery bag; it's made from oil. Don't buy a dog; pets consume natural resources. Use cloth diapers instead of disposables. Wait! Don't! They require more water and energy than Pampers.* Clearly, making eco-conscious day-to-day decisions can be a confounding process. And now there's even a term to describe the resulting condition: eco-anxiety.

If you're familiar with my "Worst-Case Scenario" series of survival handbooks, you know that anxiety is a topic with which I'm intimately familiar. But—at least in my mind—my books have always been as much about designing creative solutions as imagining serious problems. I've always strived to provide easy-to-follow survival instructions for situations where doing nothing is not an option. And today, with our climate and the planet's health—indeed, our very survival as a species—in the balance, doing nothing is the worst possible choice. It's truly not an option. Not anymore.

If you've picked up this book, you, too, realize that we need creative, environmentally responsible solutions to global warming. Fast. Like *right now*. And they need to be practical and easy to accomplish. Otherwise they won't be adopted. Some global-scale solutions that are probably inevitable, like a tax on carbon emissions, can be implemented only by governments. But conservation begins at home. The green home projects in this book are ones specifically designed for individuals: They're mostly small, inexpensive, and quick. Obviously, the larger projects (installing geothermal heating and cooling, putting up a wind turbine) take longer and require a larger investment. But their savings—both monetary and in environmental terms—are commensurate.

Like most home-improvement manuals, this book is organized by room or area. But the great thing about greening up your home is that small changes in one room can have an outsize impact on your entire house—indeed, on your entire lifestyle and your total carbon footprint. And actually, that's part of the point: to help you see things in a "green" light and to encourage you to consider your decisions with a new, eco-friendly consciousness. Once you begin thinking about energy use in terms of conservation, I guarantee you'll find new ways to save all over the place, whether at home, at work, on the road, or on vacation. (Yes, you can still take a vacation. I give you permission. Have you considered a walking tour of the neighborhood?)

A few words about some terms used in this book. Because I don't like to throw green projects at you without some evidence as to their true savings, you'll see three sections throughout the book titled "Green Bits," "Carbon Counter," and "Eco-cheat" (see key to symbols, page 13). You'll also find references to Web sites where particular green products are available, or where you can find more information that I wasn't able to cram into the book itself (I like to save paper).

As with any book about improving your home (or your life, for that matter), not all the advice here will appeal to everyone. Some people are very handy and equally ambitious. Others just want a quick fix to reduce their energy consumption and emissions—and that's OK, because you can pick and choose your projects. (If you're not handy but you *are* ambitious, may I humbly suggest hiring a professional to install your solar array?) But *This Green House* isn't only for our inner Bob Vila. Even if you never insulate your garage door or build a composter, this book will teach you how to save energy and reduce your carbon footprint by *not* doing things—that is, through conservation. Who said you can't get something for nothing?

Mind you, you don't have to live off the grid or be an ascetic to have a green home. I'm not advocating a return to preindustrial society. (And even if I were, who'd buy that book?) You'll learn how to do all the things you do now—how to eat, sleep, work, travel, and play— more efficiently, in ways you've probably never even thought of. And you may even have fun in the process! (OK, maybe not fun. But it won't hurt. Except for the cold showers.) Most important, I hope you'll enjoy learning how to do all these things, and I hope you'll at least try to follow some of the advice here. It's good for you, and it's great for the planet.

May you have two green thumbs, eight green fingers, and neighbors that go green with envy!

—Josh Piven

A MINI GLOSSARY

CO2 is the chemical symbol for carbon dioxide, a greenhouse gas that's produced by, among other things, burning fossil fuels.

Carbon neutral is a term used to describe something in which emissions released are offset (or neutralized) by the emissions sequestered. (Biodiesel is said to be carbon neutral because the plant matter used to make it absorbs as much CO_2 as the fuel releases when it's burned.) The term is also occasionally used to describe an activity with no emissions (such as walking), though "zero emissions" is more accurate in this context.

Carbon footprint refers to the amount of emissions released into the atmosphere by performing particular tasks, individually or in combination: driving a car, eating a steak, flying to Paris, and so on.

Carbon offsets is a somewhat controversial concept—and one I mention sparingly in the book. It refers to an "eco-credit" that's purchased to counteract the emissions produced by a particular activity. Many Web sites sell offsets in the form of x number of trees planted to sequester emissions equal to those produced by carrying one traveler to one destination. (My opinion is that offsets are little more than a moral balm—and that you're better off saving energy in other ways. Then again, planting a tree never hurts.) If you want to learn more, I recommend www.cdmgoldstandard.org.

Recyclable should be obvious.

Renewable, not to be confused with recyclable, refers to something (usually a natural resource) that's not destroyed or depleted when it's used, as fossil fuels are.

KEY TO SYMBOLS USED THROUGHOUT THE BOOK

GREEN BITS: Useful tips that can make a project go faster and more smoothly, further information that can help you once the project's finished, and historical "green" tidbits that give the project some perspective.

CARBON COUNTER: Facts and figures on real-world energy and resource usage (and emissions) in historical, current, and future terms.

ECO-CHEAT: Just as it sounds: ways to cut corners to accomplish a project more quickly. Keep in mind that eco-cheats typically cost more than following the project's instructions—but then time is money, too.

WARNING: Alerts you to possible dangers and hazards of a project.

CHAPTER 1

THE KITCHEN
Eat Local

Cover that pot! Turn off that water! Don't open that oven door! Yes, everything your wise old aunt—or your live-in chef—told you about cooking efficiently is true (except for the watched pot; it *will* boil—eventually). All these green tips and dozens more are expanded and explained in this chapter, which offers lots of projects that range from no-brainer (keep the coils of your refrigerator clean) to, well, those requiring a brain (capturing your sink's gray water). In between, you'll learn how to wash dishes the right way, how to reuse all those plastic bags, and how to cook dinner in your fireplace—and no, it's not just roasting marshmallows.

REDUCE ENERGY DEMANDS

FRIDGE

- Keep it full. Chilled items help keep the inside of your refrigerator cold, so the unit doesn't have to work as hard to regulate temperature each time the door is opened. Don't put hot items in the fridge, since they make the motor work harder; let hot foods cool before refrigeration.

- Buy a new one. Although fridges can last decades, new ones use up to 60 percent less energy than twenty-year-old models. Consider purchasing a model with a bottom or top freezer; side-by-side units are less efficient.

- Vacuum the coils once a month to improve efficiency by up to 30 percent.

- Don't refrigerate uncovered foods: They make the motor work harder.

The old saw about saving money by running appliances at night is still true. Kind of. But it's less true than it used to be, and it depends on how your utility company calculates your rates. If, in addition to a "generation" charge and a "transmission" charge, your bill includes a "demand" charge, this means you're charged more for demanding energy at peak times. If you have this charge, it's cheaper to spread your energy use throughout the day and night—and especially at night, when your air conditioner isn't working as hard.

OVEN/RANGE

- Install it away from your refrigerator; the oven's heat makes your fridge work harder.

- Keep the door closed. Each opening drops the temperature by 25°F.

- Use glass or ceramic pans. They're just as effective as metal ones and allow you to reduce cooking temperature by twenty-five degrees.

- Use a toaster oven for small dishes or portions. A convection toaster is even more efficient.

- When using the self-cleaning feature, turn it on right after cooking, while the oven is still hot.

- During the winter, leave the oven door open when you're finished cooking to help heat the room.

- Use a pressure cooker whenever possible. It can reduce energy consumption by 50 percent compared to an oven.

- Turn off electric heating appliances early. The heating elements on an electric stove retain heat and can be turned off ten minutes before cooking is complete.

- Keep it clean. Clean, shiny cooktop surfaces reflect heat better—and thus cook faster—than dirty, blackened ones.

DISHWASHER

- Scrape plates but don't rinse them; dishwashers are more efficient in water usage than hand washing. If you must rinse heavily soiled dishes, use cold water.

- The rinse-hold feature uses three to seven gallons of water and is usually unnecessary, especially for small loads.

- Don't run the dishwasher unless it's full.

- Turn off the dishwasher after the final rinse and open the door slightly to allow the dishes to air dry.

- If you must place your dishwasher next to your refrigerator, install a layer of foam insulation between them.

- Use as little soap as possible.

MICROWAVE

- Microwaves use lots of energy. However, they use 50–65 percent less electricity on average than ovens for cooking the same amount of food, owing to reduced cooking times.

- Microwaves work best for small portions, or for defrosting.

- Microwaves don't heat up the kitchen, potentially reducing the demands on your air-conditioning.

- Some kitchen building materials are more effective in retaining the ambient temperature, which can reduce your energy bills. These include terra-cotta (it's available recycled) and soapstone.

- The average household has its lights on in the kitchen more than in any other room save the den. Install compact fluorescent lightbulbs (CFLs) in all fixtures except the one directly over the sink: It will be exposed to steam, which isn't recommended for CFLs.

- Light-colored cabinetry and flooring will reduce the need for artificial light.

- Bamboo is an eco-friendly choice for flooring and cabinets, because cutting it doesn't kill the plant. Cork, often used for flooring, is also a renewable resource, though it's expensive.

COOK A MEAL IN YOUR FIREPLACE
ROAST CHICKEN, FIREBOX POTATOES, AND MANTEL GREEN BEANS

If you're building a fire anyway, you can save the energy needed to heat your oven by cooking an entire meal in your fireplace. For best results, consider using natural wood charcoal instead of cordwood; it burns hotter, longer, and more evenly. Avoid charcoal briquettes and manufactured synthetic logs.

MATERIALS	$0, assuming necessary materials are on hand

- ☐ 2-inch steel hook
- ☐ Cooking string or twine soaked in water
- ☐ Pan for drippings
- ☐ One large stockpot filled with 8 cups of cold, salted water
- ☐ Barbecue mitts
- ☐ Metal spoon
- ☐ Tongs or strainer
- ☐ Grill rack from oven
- ☐ Bricks or cinder blocks
- ☐ 18-inch barbecue tongs
- ☐ Aluminum foil (optional)
- ☐ Dryer lint
- ☐ Meat thermometer

INGREDIENTS	$18

- ☐ Small fryer chicken (about 3 pounds)
- ☐ 3 tablespoons butter
- ☐ ¼ cup olive oil
- ☐ Rosemary sprigs or grill brush, for basting
- ☐ Salt and pepper, to taste
- ☐ 2 pounds of green beans, washed, ends trimmed
- ☐ Four russet or eight organic Yukon Gold potatoes

STEPS TO MAKE ROAST CHICKEN

1. Screw the steel hook into the mantel, approximately 1 foot above the opening of the firebox. Alternatively, you can avoid putting a hole in the wall by tying the string or twine to a heavy object (such as a dumbbell) on the mantel and suspending the chicken from that.

2. Start the fire, using dryer lint (see "Clean Your Dryer's Exhaust Tube," page 103).

3. Remove the giblets from chicken cavity and discard, or cook separately and use them to make pâté.

4. Rinse the chicken, inside and out. Pat dry.

5. Using your hands, rub the butter all over the chicken, inside and out.

6. Sprinkle the chicken with salt and pepper.

7. Tie the legs together securely with the string.

8. Place the drippings pan directly below the hook.

9. Check the fire. Fireplace cooking isn't an exact science, of course. But like a traditional grill, the fire is hot enough for cooking when a hand placed 6 inches from it cannot be held there for more than a second or two. You can also place an oven thermometer in front of (but not directly on) the fire to measure temperature.

10. Using a slipknot, tie the free end of the string to the hook so the chicken is hanging in front of the fire, directly over the drippings pan.

11. Cook the chicken, turning and basting occasionally with drippings and/or olive oil, until the skin begins to brown. Loosen the knot, reverse the chicken so the other side is facing the fire, and repeat, adding fuel to the fire when necessary. When a meat thermometer placed into the thickest part of the thigh reads 180°F, the chicken is done. Remove and carve. Cooking time will vary with the intensity of the fire, but a small fryer chicken will take about 90 minutes.

- Don't make a fire in the fireplace *just* to cook food; the power you draw to run your oven creates fewer emissions overall.

- If you never use your fireplace, plug it and seal your chimney.

- Keep the damper (flue) closed whenever the fireplace isn't in use.

- When using the fireplace, open the lower damper, if present. If not, close all doors to the room and open the closest window about one inch, to improve airflow.

- Use grates made of C-shaped metal tubing to draw cool air into the fireplace and circulate warm air back into the room.

STEPS TO MAKE FIREBOX POTATOES

1. Soak potatoes in cold water for 15 minutes to reduce burning.

2. Make a pile of bricks or cinder blocks, about 18 inches high, on each side of the firebox.

3. Lay the grill rack across the bricks or blocks so it's level.

4. Light the fire. Wait until the wood is glowing but not flaming.

5. Place the potatoes on the rack. Optionally, wrap them in foil to reduce singeing.

6. Cook, rotating occasionally, for about 1 hour, or until a knife cuts through a potato with no resistance.

Note: The potatoes may be cooked while the chicken roasts, provided there's enough room in the fireplace.

STEPS TO MAKE MANTEL BEANS

1. Place a pot of water on the rack over a flaming fire. Bring to a boil.

2. Place the green beans in the pot. Boil, stirring occasionally with the spoon held by mitted hands, until the beans are soft but not spongy, about 8 minutes. Remove them with tongs, or strain them.

3. Rinse the beans quickly under cool water to stop the cooking process.

HAND-WASH DISHES USING LESS WATER

When it comes to cleaning dishes, dishwashers are many times more water-efficient than hand-washing with running water. However, not everybody has a dishwasher, and some items—pots and pans, typically—require soaking and scrubbing. The following hand-washing tips can help you save more than one hundred gallons of water per month.

IF YOU HAVE A DOUBLE SINK, CLOSE BOTH DRAINS

Move the faucet to hot and fill one side with the water as it warms up. This side is for rinsing. When the water begins to get warm, fill the other side, adding a minimal amount of detergent to the water. This side is for washing. If you don't have a double sink, fill a bus pan for rinsing.

LET DISHES SIT IN SUDSY WATER FOR A FEW MINUTES

This actually gets them cleaner than scrubbing them under running water, because the soap has more time to degrease them.

MORE DETERGENT EQUALS MORE WATER NEEDED TO REMOVE IT

For a standard load of dishes, one tablespoon of dishwashing liquid should be more than sufficient.

ORGANIZE THE DIRTIES

Wash dishes in the following order: glasses, utensils, plates, pots and pans. For stubborn baked-on foods, allow pots and pans to sit in soapy water overnight (except cast iron, which rusts).

SPRAY

If you must wash using running water, use the sink's sprayer hose instead of the faucet.

COMPOST INSTEAD OF USING THE GARBAGE DISPOSAL

See "Build a Composter" on page 164.

- An average load of dishes washed by hand with running water uses twenty gallons; the average dishwasher uses fifteen gallons per load—for three times the dishes.

- Washing vegetables in a pan or bowl instead of under running water can save as much as twenty gallons.

- Just 1 percent of the earth's water is fresh and available for consumption, 2 percent is frozen (for now, at least), and the rest is salt water.

CURE MEAT

The process of curing (drying) meats with salt is almost as old as humanity itself. Our mastodon-gnawing ancestors probably had access to salt before they discovered fire, and those cool, dry caves made perfect curing houses. Today, properly—and safely—curing meat requires energy (in the form of refrigeration) only in its earliest steps. After that, nature takes over. The trick to proper curing is threefold: temperature, humidity, and time.

MATERIALS	$10

- ☐ Very large, covered glass container for initial refrigeration
- ☐ Twine, for hanging the meat
- ☐ Cool basement (with optional dehumidifier, based on the season)

INGREDIENTS	Cost varies, depending on type of meat

- ☐ 2–10 pounds of fresh raw meat cleaned and rinsed; consider pork belly (to make tesa), hog jowl (to make guanciale), or a beefsteak (to make Armenian basterma)
- ☐ ½ cup kosher salt per 2 pounds of meat
- ☐ Assorted spices (optional); these may include black and white pepper, thyme, rosemary, sage, dried juniper berries, allspice berries, cumin, paprika, and anything else you think might flavor the meat well

STEPS TO CURE MEAT

1. Dry the meat thoroughly with paper towels.

2. Mix the appropriate amount of salt with the desired spices.

3. Coat the meat completely with the salt mixture, using your hands to rub it into all nooks and crannies of the flesh. This step is crucial, and it's critical that no uncoated flesh be exposed to the air.

4. Place the meat in the glass container. (Optionally, place a weight—a large, flat-bottomed bowl filled with water works well—on top of the meat.) Cover the container. Leave it in the refrigerator for about a week, turning the meat once per day. The salt will combine with the liquid in the flesh and begin to break down the enzymes that would normally produce the bacteria that lead to spoilage. Empty the liquid from the container as necessary.

5. Remove the salt-coated meat from the refrigerator and pat it dry, leaving the salt in place and adding more to any exposed areas. (For basterma, rinse the salt off, soak the meat for an hour in cold water, dry it, then follow the steps below.)

6. Check temperature, humidity, and ventilation. The basement should be less than 60°F, have a humidity level of about 65 percent, and have some air circulating. In the fall and winter, the natural air will probably be sufficiently dry. If curing in spring or summer, consider a dehumidifier with a digital humidity control. Circulating air will aid the curing process. Open a window slightly, or use a small room fan.

7. Tie the twine around the meat and hang it from a ceiling beam. Don't place the meat on any surface; it's critical that all sides of it be exposed to the air. Hanging the meat will also reduce the chances it will be discovered by vermin.

8. Wait two to four weeks.

9. Cut down the meat, wash the salt off, and enjoy.

Up until refrigeration became common, meat was either smoked or salt cured, the only ways to reliably preserve it for extended periods. Even with the advent of block ice and home iceboxes, fresh meat would not keep for more than a few days before going rancid. During the age of sail, meat was often packed in salt and stored in barrels, where it would keep indefinitely—or at least until the rats gnawed through the barrels.

REUSE YOUR SINK'S GRAY WATER

"Gray water" refers to household wastewater from sinks, dishwashers, showers and bathtubs, and clothes washers—it's distinct from "black water," or toilet waste. Although there are many potential uses for gray water, typically the only one approved in the United States is for below-the-soil plant or crop irrigation.

MATERIALS	$50

- ☐ PVC pipe, threaded at both ends, cut to fit the distance from the sink to the storage tank
- ☐ PVC U-joint with couplings, sized to accept the pipe
- ☐ Two PVC J-joints with couplings, sized to accept the pipe
- ☐ Food-grade 55-gallon plastic storage drum, with a tight-fitting lid
- ☐ Keyhole saw or matte knife
- ☐ Plumber's wrench
- ☐ Drill and masonry bit
- ☐ Caulk
- ☐ 5 percent chlorine bleach (optional)
- ☐ Male pipe thread to garden hose thread coupling, with flange (optional)
- ☐ Hose (optional)

STEPS TO REUSE GRAY WATER

1. Using the saw or knife, cut a hole in the lid of the storage tank to accept the J-joint. It should fit snugly with no play.

2. Under the sink, use the plumber's wrench to disconnect the drainpipe where the U-joint (the "trap") meets the straight section.

3. Drill a hole from the rear of the cabinet under the sink through your home's exterior wall. Use a masonry bit, if necessary, and widen the hole to the diameter of the PVC pipe.

4. Replace the sink's existing U-joint with the PVC J-joint, connect the curved end of one of the J-joints to the U-joint, then connect the gray-water PVC pipe to the other side of the J-joint. The pipe should be long enough to carry the gray water outside your home and supply the storage tank. It should be level or angled downward a few degrees. Caulk around the pipe where it passes through the wall.

5. Connect the second J-joint to the other end of the pipe.

6. Insert the other end of the J-joint through the hole in the top of the storage tank.

- Add a screen or mesh filter just below the lid to catch and separate large food particles from the gray water. This step isn't necessary—large particles will settle to the bottom of the tank eventually—but it saves time. However, exposed food particles may invite insects and other pests.

- Cut a hole approximately 1 foot above the bottom of the tank and install the hose coupling (see "Capture and Reuse Rainwater," page 154).

- Disinfect the water using 1.8 milliliters of liquid bleach per 10 gallons of water. Note that in most cases this isn't necessary, and it may be detrimental to plant growth.

- Gray water constitutes 50–80 percent of all residential wastewater.

- In municipalities with combined sewage systems, gray water and black water are mixed at the sewer and sent to water treatment plants. By reducing your gray water output, you'll be putting less stress on these facilities.

7. Allow water to settle for several hours, then remove it using a bucket or by attaching a garden hose. Remove any settled material and flush it down the toilet.

8. Apply water to soil. It shouldn't touch exposed areas of plants.

- Gray water should be used within twenty-four hours or discarded.

- Wear rubber gloves when handling gray water.

- There has never been a documented case of illness linked to gray water.

- In a direct (unfiltered, untreated) gray-water system, nothing toxic should go down your drain, including bleaches, dyes, bath salts, chemical cleansers, and nonbiodegradable soaps. If you can't pronounce the ingredients, don't use it.

- Gray water is not safe for drinking, bathing, or hand washing. Its collection is regulated by varying state laws, and do-it-yourself systems like this one may be illegal in some places.

- Don't use gray water where it may seep into wells.

MAKE COFFEE-GROUND CHARCOAL

This homemade alternative contains fewer chemicals than store-bought briquettes and eliminates manufacturing and shipping costs. Plus, because coffee grounds contain more oil and less char and carbon, they burn hotter and longer than wood.

MATERIALS	$20 (plus coffee)

- ☐ 5 pounds of used coffee grounds
- ☐ Newspaper (for drying them)
- ☐ 2 ½ pounds of candle wax chips (beeswax preferred)
- ☐ Candy thermometer
- ☐ Double boiler
- ☐ Narrow, loaf-type baking pan
- ☐ Cooking spray
- ☐ One piece of scrap plywood, cut to fit snugly inside the top of the baking pan
- ☐ Hacksaw
- ☐ Bench vise (optional)

STEPS TO MAKE CHARCOAL

1. Spread the damp grounds evenly on several sheets of newspaper. Allow to dry in the sun until no dampness remains.

2. Melt about ½ pound of beeswax chips in a double boiler until the wax reaches 160°F. Warning: Do not let the wax get any hotter or it may ignite!

3. Remove wax from heat. Stir in several cups of the dried grounds until the mixture has the consistency of oatmeal.

4. Pour the mixture into a greased baking pan.

5. Place the piece of wood on top of your coffee-ground-and-wax loaf. Place the baking pan into the optional vise, with one end on the bottom of the pan and the other on top of the wood. Tighten the vise. If you don't have a vise, weigh down the wood with several dumbbells or a large pot filled with water.

6. Allow to cool overnight.

7. Remove the loaf from the pan. You may need to rap sharply on the bottom to dislodge it. Repeat Steps 1–7 with the remaining wax and grounds.

8. Using the saw, cut the loaf crosswise into 1-inch "slices." Flip the loaf on its side, make one cut, then cut the remaining sections into 2-inch blocks.

9. Use it as you would charcoal, lighting it with a charcoal starter or balled newspaper. Most of the wax should burn off, but consider placing the coffee ground blocks in a cast iron pan to catch any melted wax.

You can use an uncut coffee-ground log in the fireplace as a substitute for manufactured "sawdust" logs.

BUILD A TERRA-COTTA FLOWERPOT GRILL

It takes less than $20 and only ten minutes to turn a spare flowerpot into a grill. If you use hardwood charcoal as a heat source, your grill will be effectively carbon neutral: The trees used to make the charcoal absorbed more CO_2 than burning wood releases.

MATERIALS	$15

- ☐ Large, thick terra-cotta pot, at least 14 inches in diameter
- ☐ Grill grate, 12 inches in diameter or smaller
- ☐ Two bricks
- ☐ Sand
- ☐ Charcoal
- ☐ Terra-cotta saucer of equal or larger diameter (optional)

!

WARNING: Keep this grill out of the reach of children.

STEPS TO BUILD GRILL

1. Place bricks on a stone surface, then place the pot on the bricks. The bricks act as external heat sinks, keeping the bottom of the pot from getting too hot and potentially cracking. Don't place bricks on a wood surface.

2. Fill the pot with about 3 inches of sand. The sand acts as an internal heat sink.

3. Place charcoal on the sand and ignite it. Consider using a metal charcoal cylinder instead of lighter fluid to help ignite the coals.

4. When the coals are hot, lower the grill grate into the pot until it wedges firmly against the sides.

5. Grill normally.

6. Place the saucer upside down on top of the pot to cut off oxygen and extinguish the coals when finished.

Note: The sides of the pot will get very hot, and they may remain so for hours. Do not light your terra-cotta pot grill if the outside temperature is very cold, or it may crack.

STEP 1

STEP 4

Although packaged charcoal briquettes are not as environmentally friendly as natural charcoal, they produce less ash, tend to burn more evenly, and don't burn as hot, and therefore they can be substituted for natural (lump) charcoal in this situation.

MAKE A PLASTIC BAG DRYER

The U.S. Environmental Protection Agency (EPA) estimates that we consume 380 billion plastic bags each year—and a staggering one trillion are used worldwide. While you can easily replace grocery store–supplied plastic bags with your own reusable ones, zipper closure–type bags used in the kitchen don't always have an easy substitute. Consider the following steps as an alternative to throwing them away.

METHOD ONE
MAKE THE OUTSIDE DRYER

MATERIALS	$5

- ☐ Dish soap
- ☐ Sponge
- ☐ Bus pan for rinsing
- ☐ Clothesline and clothespins

1. Turn bags inside out. Place 1/4 teaspoon of eco-friendly dish soap into a sink filled with warm water. Agitate the water. Place the bags into the sink and scrub gently with a sponge. Rinse bags in the bus pan. Shake dry.

2. Using clothespins, clip the bags to the clothesline and allow to air-dry outside.

METHOD TWO
MAKE THE INDOOR DRYER

MATERIALS	$5

- ☐ Dish soap
- ☐ Sponge
- ☐ Bus pan
- ☐ Ten to twelve metal or wood skewers, or drinking straws
- ☐ Mixing bowl filled with sand, dried beans, or popcorn kernels

1. Wash bags (see Method 1, Step 1).

2. Stick the skewers into the sand-filled bowl to about the 4-inch mark, or until they stay upright. They should be angled slightly, not straight up and down.

3. Place a damp bag, wet side out, onto a skewer. Repeat with the other bags. Allow them to dry overnight.

In March 2002, Ireland introduced the "PlasTax," the equivalent of a 20-cent-per-bag tax on plastic bags; their use declined by 95 percent.

STEP
1

STEP
2

STEP
3

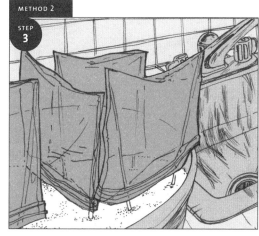

- Traditional plastic bags do not biodegrade. Instead, they photodegrade, breaking down into tiny plastic bits that can contaminate soil and groundwater, foul oceans, and harm marine life—pretty much forever.

- Do not wash and reuse plastic bags that have held raw foods. Instead, use ceramic or glass containers with lids.

- Do not reuse a bag that is discolored.

- Bags that have held dry goods or fresh vegetables can simply be rinsed.

- Label bags (lettuce, carrots, broccoli) so you can reuse them for the same items. Avoid storing cut onions in plastic bags.

- Cheeses can be wrapped in recyclable parchment paper and stored in airtight containers.

- Do not wash plastic bags in the dishwasher.

31

REUSE PLASTIC WATER BOTTLES

21 NEW USES

The plastic water bottle has become the contemporary equivalent of the curbside aluminum can of the 1970s: a total and needless waste of natural resources. Follow these tips to make useful items from your empty bottles.

CAT TOY

Place a few dried navy or kidney beans in a bottle. Cap it. Give it to a cat to knock around. Alternately, tie one end of a string to the bottle and the other end to a stick. Hold the stick and watch the cat swat at the bottle.

WET PAINTED-NAIL PROTECTOR

Insert each finger into the neck of an empty bottle until your nails are dry. Do not attempt to drive a car, operate heavy machinery, or type.

SHORT-TERM WINE STORAGE

Pour any unused wine into an empty plastic bottle, to the very top. Tighten the cap. The wine will keep, refrigerated, for a week or more. (Note: Although you can use plastic, glass bottles are preferable for wine storage.) Plastic bottles are also excellent for storage of raw rice—use a funnel to get the rice into the bottle.

BARBELL

Fill ten empty bottles with sand or gravel. Cap them. Using twine, tie five bottles to each end of a stout rod or dowel. Use as you would a barbell, to do curls or to bench-press.

BABY RATTLE

Fill a plastic bottle with popcorn kernels or dried beans. Tighten the top and wrap it with tape.

MOBILE

Fill four bottles of the same size with colored strips of tissue paper. Poke holes in the caps and tie them to two wood skewers, one on each end. Tie or tape the skewers together to make an X and hang it from the ceiling.

TELEPHONE

Cut the bottoms off two bottles. Tie the narrow ends together with ten feet of yarn. Speak and listen through the wider end. (Note: More than ten feet of yarn may result in poor reception.)

SUBMARINE

Using a metal skewer or awl, poke ten holes in the sides of the top half of a bottle. Place it in a bathtub or pool. As the bottle fills with water, it will "dive" to the bottom. Use a colored bottle for an added effect.

FUNNEL

Cut off the bottom four inches of the bottle. Use the remainder as a funnel.

VASE

Pour two inches of gravel or pebbles into the bottle. Fill it with water and use as a vase, especially for tulips and Gerber daisies.

MEAT TENDERIZER

Fill a bottle with water, dried beans, or popcorn kernels. Cap it. Cover meat with plastic wrap, then smack the bottle against it to tenderize.

SCREW, NUT, AND BOLT STORAGE

Cut bottles in half. Use the bottom halves to organize workshop items.

PLANT STARTERS

Cut bottles in half. Poke a few holes in the bottom halves for drainage. Fill them with soil and add seeds or young plants.

PUTTING HOLE

Cut off the top two-thirds of the bottle. Place the bottom third on its side, with the opening facing your tee. Putt a golf ball into the bottle. The bottle should pop upright when (and if) the ball lands in it.

BIRD FEEDER

Cut a hole the size of a dime just above the bottom edge of the bottle. Tape or glue a pencil to the bottom of the bottle to serve as a perch. Fill the bottle with birdseed, tighten the cap, and hang it outside the window with string.

CHECKERS AND CHESS

Remove the caps. Paint them, and use them as checkers. Paint or label empty bottles and use them as super-size chess pieces.

LAWN BOWLING PINS

Fill ten bottles with two inches of popcorn kernels each. Use them with a rubber ball for lawn (or family room) bowling.

BEVERAGE COOLER

Fill a bottle with water, leaving one inch of room at the top. Cap it. Freeze the bottle, then use it to chill beverages in an insulated bag. Warning: Do not drink the water in the bottle after it thaws. Refreeze the water, or discard it and refill the bottle.

FISHING BOBBER

Wrap a fishing line around the neck of a capped bottle, leaving several feet hanging down. Secure it with a knot. Tie a fishhook to the free end.

"JUST MARRIED!" ORNAMENT

Tie a dozen empty bottles to the bumper of a car driven by newlyweds. Note: The sound will be slightly more subdued, unless the bottles are filled with rice or raw corn kernels.

POOL FLOAT

Fill a sturdy plastic garbage bag with as many empty bottles as you can find (make sure the caps are secure). Tie the bag closed. Use as a chair or lounger. Tie ten filled bags together to make a "recycled island."

- Americans buy more than four billion gallons of water per year in individual-portion bottles.

- Twenty-nine billion plastic bottles are produced for use in the United States each year. Manufacturing them requires the equivalent of seventeen million barrels of oil.

- The United States spends $43 billion per year to produce clean, safe tap water.

- Bottled water can cost $10 per gallon; tap water costs a penny a gallon.

- One-quarter of all bottled water travels across national borders before being consumed.

- In the United States alone, the energy used for pumping, processing, transporting, and refrigerating bottled water produces an annual "fossil fuel footprint" of fifty million barrels of oil—enough to run three million cars for a year.

- Plastic bottle caps are typically not recyclable.

Less than 25 percent of plastic bottles produced are recycled.

CHAPTER 2

THE FAMILY ROOM
Energy Conservation

You've had a long day. So sit back. Relax. And then ponder how that Jumbotron you call a television is killing the planet. These days, the family room—the place where most people go to relax and conserve energy—uses almost as much energy as the kitchen. Huge TVs. DVD players. Burning-hot cable boxes. Fifty speakers. Computers. The control room at NASA has fewer lights and plugs. Fortunately, you can start to green up your power-hungry den by taking some baby steps first (changing the settings on your equipment, using rechargeable batteries), then moving on to making recycled furniture and dealing with energy loss. Only then can you relax on your foam-peanut couch and put your feet up on your coffee-can coffee table.

MAKE A CABLE BOX TOWEL WARMER

Your cable box is one of the most eco-unfriendly appliances in your home. The average digital set-top box is in standby mode (not actively being used) 78 percent of the time—yet its power draw is a constant twenty-three watts. A cable box in a glass-enclosed cabinet can reach temperatures approaching 100°F—more than warm enough to perform double duty as a towel warmer.

MATERIALS	$0, except for the cost of the energy used to heat the box

- ☐ Cable (or satellite) box
- ☐ Wire oven rack
- ☐ Four clean, empty aluminum cans
- ☐ Bath towel

STEPS TO MAKE THE WARMER

1. Preheat box. Make sure it's plugged in and receiving power. Close the cabinet doors, if they're present. Watch television for 10–15 minutes, if desired.

2. Position cans. Place one, closed end up, at each corner of the cable box. Use smaller, pet food–type cans for a warmer towel.

3. Place the oven rack on the cans.

4. Place the folded towel on the rack.

5. Wait 10 minutes, turning it once.

6. Enjoy the warmed towel.

- If current trends continue, by 2010 the electricity used by set-top boxes in the United States could approach 4 percent of total residential electricity use.

- A digital cable box uses more than twice the energy of an analog box. A high-definition box uses more than a standard digital one, and in some cases more than some televisions. Some digital video recorders have no power switch and consume sixty watts of power all the time.

- Set-top boxes currently installed in the United States consume twenty terawatts (twenty trillion watts) per year, or 13 percent of the total electricity consumed by consumer electronic devices, not including digital TVs.

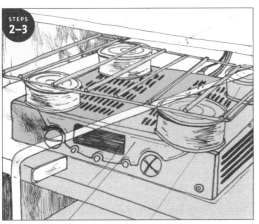

CONSTRUCT RECYCLED FURNITURE
TIN CAN COFFEE TABLE, FOAM PEANUT COUCH, AND NEWSPAPER OTTOMAN

Typical home furnishings are environmentally unfriendly. They use nonrecycled, old-growth hardwoods, chemically treated fibers, and metals that pollute when extracted or smelted. Add in the carbon costs of transporting all those La-Z-Boys, and you've got a living room set ripe for a little greening. The following furniture can be made using common household items, a little time, and some ingenuity.

COFFEE CAN TABLE

A nice coffee table is always a good conversation piece. Imagine the conversations that a homemade coffee can table will provoke! You'll also be saving money by drinking Folgers instead of Starbucks for a few months as you collect your cans.

In terms of emissions, are you better off recycling those cans and buying a new coffee table? Only if the purchased coffee table is made from recycled aluminum. And don't forget, the cans from your coffee table are still recyclable later. Consider:

- Recycling aluminum creates 97 percent less water pollution than producing new metal from ore.

- Recycling one ton of aluminum saves the equivalent in energy of 2,350 gallons of gasoline or of the amount of electricity used by the typical home over ten years.

- Recycling one aluminum can saves enough energy to run an energy-burning television for three hours.

STEPS TO MAKE THE TABLE

1. Sand the edges of the wood until they're smooth. If you're worried about stains, apply two coats of varnish. (Coasters are more eco-friendly.) This is the top of the table.

2. Place four of the cans on the ground, upside down (bottoms up). Position the wood so the cans are at the corners. Drill four holes, one at each corner, through the wood and the center of each can.

3. Place the top on its edge and push the bolts through it. Thread the bolts through the cans. Using pliers, tighten the nuts and washers inside the cans. You should now have the top secured to four cans, making a tatami-style coffee table that's too low to use—unless you prefer to sit on the floor.

4. For each leg, apply a coat of contact cement or epoxy around the bottom edge (closed end) of one of the remaining cans, then press the top (open end) of another can onto it. You should now have four sets of two attached cans. Allow them to dry overnight.

5. Finally, apply the glue to the exposed bottom edge of each can, as in Step 4, then press the coffee-table top—with its attached cans—onto those four sets of cans. You should now have a coffee-can coffee table, with three cans at each corner supporting the top.

MATERIALS	$30

- ☐ Twelve large aluminum coffee cans, emptied of coffee
- ☐ Contact cement or epoxy
- ☐ One 4-x-4-foot sheet of scrap wood
- ☐ Four ¾-inch bolts, with nuts and washers
- ☐ Drill
- ☐ Pliers
- ☐ Sandpaper
- ☐ Varnish (optional)

Note: Aluminum cans have incredible strength. For a heavier, sturdier table, consider using unopened coffee cans for the bottom two sections of each leg—or stacks of six-packs. (When you run out of beer during the big game, you can cannibalize the table.)

Aluminum never wears out; it can be recycled forever.

FOAM "PEANUT" COUCH

Most couches are replaced when their cushions—
the stuffing—become compacted, not because of
frame failure. You can easily revive the cushions
with one of the most commonly used (and environmentally deleterious) packing materials: foam
peanuts. Further, the newer type of biodegradable
peanuts can be replaced and recycled indefinitely.

STEPS TO MAKE THE COUCH

1. Remove sofa cushions. Unzip covers and
   machine- or hand-wash them (depending on
   care instructions) in cold water. Air-dry. Don't
   tumble dry, or the covers may shrink.

2. Examine the cushion stuffing. Most sofas are
   stuffed with either foam or a combination of
   foam, cotton, and down (feathers). Consider
   using the old cushions as makeshift mattresses for guests. Another excellent use is to
   place them under the thin, uncomfortable
   mattress of a sofa bed, for added cushioning.
   (Use them only when the bed is unfolded.)
   You can also cut the foam into strips and use it
   around window air conditioners, as insulation.

3. Determine the type of foam peanut you have.
   Hold one between your thumb and forefinger. Squeeze gently. If it compacts to almost
   flat, it's probably a biodegradable cornstarch
   or sorghum peanut. If it retains its shape, it's
   most likely true foam (polystyrene). To be certain, hold the peanut under running water. If
   it begins to dissolve, it's biodegradable.

MATERIALS	$0, if you collect peanuts $25, if you buy them new

- ☐ Packing peanuts (lots)
- ☐ Old couch

4. Fill sofa cushions with peanuts. Zip closed,
   then place them on the couch. True foam
   peanuts will hold their shape and last forever,
   but they tend to squeak as they compact. Biodegradable peanuts will be more comfortable,
   but they'll become highly compacted over
   time and require replacement. Avoid spilling
   liquids on a cornstarch-peanut couch, or the
   cushions will shrink.

A 2004 study found that in the categories
of energy consumption, greenhouse gas
emissions, and total negative effects, polystyrene's environmental impact was the
second highest. And first? Aluminum.

NEWSPAPER OTTOMAN

This is one of the easiest pieces of recycled furniture to construct. What's more, newspaper ottomans can be resized easily. And if you get a daily paper (a physical one; online doesn't count), you should be able to amass the necessary newsprint in less than a month.

MATERIALS	$2, not including the cost of newspapers

☐ Newspapers
☐ Twine
☐ Scissors

STEPS TO MAKE THE OTTOMAN

1. Stack newspapers to the desired height; a typical ottoman or footstool is 17–18 inches high. (Two complete Sunday newspapers piled one atop of the other should be about 4 inches high.)

2. Unspool approximately 10 feet of twine. Cut.

3. Slide the twine under the stack, bring the ends together on top, then cross them and pull taut, as you would wrapping a box with ribbon. Bring the loose ends down the remaining two sides.

4. Holding the twine tightly, flip the newspaper stack upside down and tie off the twine on the bottom, cutting off any excess.

5. Flip the ottoman back over and rest your feet. If the papers slide, cut the twine, wrap the corners of the stack first with the flaps from a cardboard box, then retie the stack using fresh twine.

- The tanning process, used to make furniture- and clothing-grade leather, is highly dependent on chemicals.

- Modern tanning techniques are high in chromium IV, a known carcinogen.

- Leather is a by-product industry, dependent on the world's consumption of meat for its survival. Biodegradable foam peanuts are edible, but they may cause bloating.

- A cornstarch-peanut couch may be attractive to pets and rodents.

- Polystyrene is highly flammable.

- Polystyrene takes approximately nine hundred years to decompose.

MAKE YOUR WINDOWS MORE ENERGY EFFICIENT

One-third of a typical home's energy loss is through doors and windows—and your home has lots more windows than doors. Ideally, you'd replace all your old windows with new, double-paned glass windows that sandwich an insulating gas such as argon. But this is expensive. The following tips are much cheaper and easier to implement, and they can lower your utility bills significantly.

CAULK

Caulking is by far the cheapest and easiest way to seal drafty windows. Fill in all visible cracks in frames with paintable caulk, then paint. For large gaps, seal with Spackle or wood filler, then paint. Alternatively, you can use self-stick foam or rolled rubber weather stripping. Estimated cost: $10.

KEEP STORM WINDOWS CLOSED MOST OF THE TIME

In winter, storm windows will help the house retain heat. In summer, they'll prevent cool air from leaking out. (You can leave them up on nice fall and spring days when your home's heating/cooling system isn't on.) Estimated cost: $0.

HANG PLASTIC SHEETING

Although it's a pain to put up and rather unsightly, the plastic sheeting in window insulation kits is a relatively inexpensive method to reduce drafts. Keep in mind, however, that it's typically single-use, and the sealer tape is often hard to remove without taking off paint. And if you don't seal it taut, it'll be flappin' in the breeze all winter long. Estimated cost: $5 per window (depending on size).

HANG INSULATED DRAPES

In winter, open them on sunny days and close them at night. In summer, close them during the day to keep the house cool. If your windows have shutters, follow the same regimen. Even blinds, when used properly, can have an effect. Estimated cost: It depends on the number and size of windows, but figure $100 per window, though not all windows will require them.

PLANT WINDOW BOXES

To get the best cooling effect, you'd mount the boxes above your windows and plant lots of hanging ivy—but this isn't really practical. However, even flowers and shrubs just a few feet high can help to block the heating rays of the sun for a few hours per day, particularly for east-, west-, and south-facing windows (north-facing in the southern hemisphere). In addition, they look nice and are eco-friendly. Strategically planted trees can also help (see "Grow Nut Trees," page 179). Estimated cost: $30 per window, including inexpensive window boxes.

USE OVERHANGS

When designing a new home, consider roof overhangs and retractable awnings, which can reduce the intensity of the sun's rays that enter windows. Use caution when choosing this option in hurricane- or tornado-prone regions. Estimated cost: It depends on construction pricing, but at least a few dollars per square foot.

- One 3-x-5-foot window with a one-sixteenth-inch gap around the sashes is like having a hole the size of a brick in your house. Ouch.

- Energy lost through residential and commercial windows costs U.S. consumers about $25 billion each year. Double ouch.

- A technology developed in Japan called "switchable glass" may make its way into green buildings in the near future. Switchable glass changes color (and even reflectivity) based on environmental conditions. Previous incarnations of this technology, including electrochromatic glass, tended to get so hot that they reradiated infrared radiation into a room; used exotic, expensive gases; or had a yellowish tint unsuitable for many applications. The new technology adds inexpensive oxygen and hydrogen between two sheets of glass, which changes its reflectivity. Scientists estimate it could offer energy savings of nearly 30 percent.

- Test the draftiness of your windows by taping long, thin strands of tissue paper to the frames. If the paper flaps, your windows and/or frames need improvements.

MAKE YOUR AUDIO/VIDEO EQUIPMENT MORE ECO-FRIENDLY

Consumer electronics account for more than 10 percent of the nation's energy consumption. From stereos and telephones to battery chargers and DVD players, virtually anything in your family room that draws power also wastes it. Of course, you're not going to purchase a carbon offset every time you watch *American Idol* (though perhaps there's an offset for your wasted time). But there are ways you can make the equipment you use more efficient. Let the following tips be your energy guide.

USE A "GREEN" POWER STRIP

This new breed of "smart" power strip has secondary outlets connected to a primary outlet. When the device—say, a computer or a TV—plugged into the primary outlet goes into standby or sleep mode, the devices drawing power from the secondary outlets are turned off. Completely. This is an excellent solution for A/V equipment without standby modes. Estimated cost: $25.

TURN OFF COMPUTER MONITORS

Memorize this phrase: "Screen savers do not save electricity." When it's not in use, turn off your computer monitor. Unless you're a programmer working all the time, turn off your PC at night when you're sleeping; the standby mode still consumes electricity.

TURN OFF MODEMS

Even when your computer is not on, your cable modem is. Turn it off when you're not using it, or at the very least when you're away on vacation. Avoid unplugging it, however, as this may require lengthy reinitialization.

INSTALL A CEILING FAN

All that fancy equipment in your family room puts out lots of heat. In summer, this means your air conditioner has to work that much harder. A ceiling fan won't lower the air temperature, but it can make a room feel several degrees cooler. Use it on high except in very humid conditions, when it should be set on a lower speed.

BUY A "GREEN" STEREO

Eco-friendly audio equipment is just beginning to become available, but it's the sound of the future. Such devices use organic light-emitting diodes (OLEDs) instead of conventional bulbs, require less than one watt of power in standby mode (which means they actually *have* a standby mode), are manufactured with low levels of heavy metals, and use recycled and recyclable packaging. Estimated cost: $300 per component.

INSTALL A HOME ENERGY MONITOR

Information is power, and more information can save power. Studies have shown that drivers of hybrid cars save fuel not only because their cars get better mileage but also because hybrids monitor and display fuel usage in real time—allowing drivers to adjust their driving behavior. The same principle is now being applied to the home with real-time energy monitors that display, each second, how much electricity you're using. This means no more waiting for (and dreading) the utility bill. Visit www.ambientdevices.com for details. Estimated cost: $200.

The average U.S. home has roughly two TVs, a VCR, a DVD player, and three telephones—and the numbers are growing. If each of these was replaced with a more efficient Energy Star model, it would save twenty-five billion pounds of greenhouse gas emissions—equivalent to taking two million cars off the road.

REDUCE REMOTE CONTROL BATTERY USAGE

Are disposable batteries really the root of all environmental (or at least landfill) evil? Well, no. And yes. Sort of. Before a law was passed in 1996 outlawing mercury in disposable batteries, they were among the worst environmental offenders in your household trash. Toxic waste, essentially. But batteries manufactured since then have been reengineered so their metals are of low enough toxicity to be safely disposed of in landfills or incinerated, at least according to the EPA. (Car batteries are another story; see below.) Still, batteries are made of metal. Eventually that metal has to go someplace, and if it's not recycled it's going to go into the air (if incinerated) or into the soil (if placed in a landfill). And that's not to mention all the natural resources used to manufacture those billions of batteries used by consumers each year. Fortunately, reducing your remote control battery usage is relatively simple. And it will save you money.

USE A "SMART" REMOTE

In this age of wondrous modern conveniences, there is really no reason to have five remote controls lying around. Typically, your cable or satellite box will include a programmable universal remote that you can use to operate all (or most) of your equipment. You may need to enter a few codes (in the worst-case scenario, you may have to call the manufacturer to get them), but you'll be saving lots of batteries. You can also purchase a smart remote for less than $20 (or more than $300, if you require one that uses lots of batteries). Of course, when you misplace the smart remote you'll really be in trouble.

- Fifteen billion batteries are produced worldwide each year.

- Lead-acid car batteries are extremely dangerous for groundwater and, by U.S. law, must be recycled. The average car built today contains twenty-seven pounds of lead, most of it in the battery.

- Replacing the batteries in a hybrid car would cost as much as replacing the engine.

- A service called "Big Green Box" will recycle virtually any type of battery in your home—including those containing mercury and lead, and those in computers. Shipping is included. See www.biggreenbox.com for details. A similar service, "Call2Recycle," is available at www.rbrc.org/call2recycle.

PROGRAM YOUR REMOTE

If you're like most people, you watch only a small fraction of the cable channels you pay for. You can reduce the battery-draining scrolling through the online guide by programming the remote to display only the channels you watch. Check the channel guide or cable menu to see how to program your favorites.

STORE BATTERIES PROPERLY

Temperature extremes—particularly heat—reduce the usable life of all batteries. Obviously, you're not going to store your remote control in the freezer. But even leaving one on the sill of an open window on a hot day can reduce the life of the batteries inside. Standard alkaline batteries self-discharge over time even when stored at room temperature, but only by a small amount per year.

DON'T LET BATTERIES SIT IDLE

As soon as you place a battery in your remote, a chemical reaction inside the battery begins that will eventually deplete it. Even if you don't use the remote again for weeks or months, eventually the batteries will die. It sounds obvious, but it's worth saying: Make sure you actually use the batteries in your remote once you insert them. Don't bother removing them to make them last longer; this won't work.

USE RECHARGEABLES

Recharging a battery is much less energy- and carbon-intensive than manufacturing a new one. It also reduces waste. What's more, under most high-drain conditions such as those found in consumer electronics, rechargeables will actually last longer than disposables. Rechargeable nickel metal hydride (NiMH) AA and AAA batteries are good choices for almost all remote controls. Their well-known downside (a fast self-discharge rate) is now being overcome with a new technology called Ultra-Low Self-Discharge. Like all rechargeables, their initial cost is higher than equally rated disposables, but they more than make up for their cost over time.

USE A SOLAR CHARGER

If you really want to go green, consider a solar charger for your rechargeable batteries. Solar chargers typically take much longer to charge a battery than a standard wall charger, and they usually require proprietary attachments—and, sometimes, special batteries. They're also about three times the cost of a standard NiMH recharger. On the bright side, the sun's available at no charge. For details visit: www.greenbatteries.com/solarproducts.html.

Whole Foods recycles cellular phone batteries.

MAKE YOUR SIXTY-INCH TELEVISION MORE EFFICIENT

The new breed of flat-panel TVs may look cool, but they run hot. Very hot. In fact, the average plasma television uses three times as much energy per screen inch as an old-style cathode-ray TV. In general, LCD TVs use less energy than plasmas—assuming identical screen size—while fifty-inch-and-larger plasmas are the biggest electricity hogs. On average, costs for running these stylish TVs range from about $13 per year at the low end to as much as $150 (which is probably much more than your refrigerator). Use the following tips to reduce your TV's energy consumption.

WATCH IT LESS

Yes, it sounds silly, but TVs use most of their energy—though not all—when they're on. One effective TV reduction strategy is to avoid channel surfing. Turn the television on only when you know there's something you want to watch. Alternatively, scroll through the digital guide only once. If you don't find anything to your liking, turn the TV off and pick up a book. Or the TV guide.

TURN DOWN FACTORY SETTINGS

Many TVs ship from the factory with their picture settings (brightness, hue, color, saturation) at their highest levels, to make them look good when compared to other brands at the store. On most units, reducing these settings (especially brightness) to the 50 percent level will give a more-than-adequate viewing experience while reducing energy consumption by as much as 15 percent.

CHECK THE TV'S ENERGY DEMANDS BEFORE YOU BUY IT

Believe it or not, flat-panel TVs of the same size—and even from the same manufacturer—don't always consume the same amount of electricity. The amount can vary by as much as two hundred watts. Read labels carefully.

ELIMINATE THE STANDBY MODE

Even when flat-panel TVs are "off," they're still on, in so-called standby mode, which uses energy (see under Carbon Counter, below). To eliminate this energy trickle, plug all your audio/video equipment into a surge protector or power strip. When the equipment isn't in use, turn the surge protector off, cutting power completely. One note of caution here: Most digital cable boxes require constant power to keep program guides current. Turning them off completely means the program guide function won't work immediately when power is restored, since program information loads slowly. To combat this annoyance, turn the cable box off at night when you go to bed and back on when you get up in the morning. The program guide will update within a few minutes. Turning it off shouldn't affect cable Internet service.

TURN OFF OR DIM ROOM LIGHTS

While admittedly this won't save on the energy your massive TV consumes, it will save you money, and it has the further benefit of adding to the perceived brightness and saturation of your television's picture. Closing blinds or pulling shades to reduce glare will also improve picture quality without forcing you to make the picture brighter.

USE INTERNAL SPEAKERS WHENEVER POSSIBLE

Your fifteen-speaker-matrix-surround-sound-keep-the-neighbors-up-all-night audio setup isn't really necessary for watching the nightly news—and it consumes energy. Consider using your TV's smaller, but still adequate, speakers when not watching movies.

- TVs and cable boxes are just two of the many "vampire appliances" that consume small amounts of energy even when they're seemingly turned off. (Feel the adapter when it's plugged in and not actively being used. If it's warm, it's drawing power.) All these small amounts add up: The average home is filled with standby energy suckers, which include electric toothbrushes, cordless phones, garage door openers, computers, satellite dishes, microwaves, and anything with a digital clock. One study has estimated that such appliances cost consumers $3 billion per year ($200 per household) and consume energy equivalent to that produced by seven power plants.

- Currently, products that consume one watt or less in standby mode are considered the most efficient available. The Web site oahu.lbl.gov has information on the standby energy usage of various products.

- Energy Star, the U.S. Department of Energy's efficiency ratings program, recently established guidelines for a new type of television that has a "digital cable ready with point of deployment" slot. Such TVs will eliminate the need for inefficient cable boxes—few of which meet Energy Star guidelines—in favor of a small card that can be inserted into the TV to perform the same functions. And you can take it with you when you move.

CHAPTER 3

THE BEDROOM
Invigorate

Because it is mostly appliance-free, your bedroom is actually among the most energy-efficient spaces in your house—unless that's where your home gym and central air-conditioning unit are located. But just because it's not filled with gear doesn't mean it can't be made more green, from the bed you sleep on to the clothes you pile on the chair to the candles you burn during a date night at home. Projects in this chapter address all these areas, as well as ideas for greening up furniture, walls, and flooring; eliminating the alarm clock; and cleaning with natural products.

CHOOSE A GREEN BED

For a truly renewable bed, you *could* sleep on a slab of sod. But a lawn is difficult to grow in your bedroom, not to mention pretty high maintenance. An eco-friendly "green" bed is the next best thing, made from sustainable resources and materials that aren't chemically treated. Keep in mind, too, that for the next ten years you'll be spending eight hours a night—more, if you're lucky—on your bed. So don't skimp.

THE MATTRESS

Fortunately, there are more green options available today than just a few years ago—and you won't be forced to choose between a metal spring mattress and a futon. Choose either 100 percent pure natural latex or a natural latex core with organic cotton and wool. Natural latex is simply rubber, from the rubber tree (*Hevea brasiliensis*). It contains no petrochemicals and is naturally hypoallergenic, antimicrobial, and resistant to dust mites. It's also very supportive, and it's 100 percent biodegradable. Note that synthetic latex is cheaper, but not a natural product. Avoid cotton-filled futon mattresses, which tend to ball and compress over time and aren't very supportive. Estimated cost: $700 and up.

THE FRAME

Obviously, anything made of wood is made from something that was cut down by someone, somewhere, at some point. Bamboo, however, is a sustainable choice, because cutting it down doesn't kill the plant. Some companies promise to use woods (typically pine) that are sustainably harvested—which means they only cut off the tops. Just kidding. They replant new trees after cutting. You'll have to take their word for it. Others construct beds using particleboard, which is scrap wood that's mixed with (typically petroleum-based) adhesive. Ecologically speaking, your best choice is to buy a used bed frame, or one constructed of reclaimed (also called "salvaged") wood or metal. If you buy it locally, you'll also be cutting down on shipping costs and pollution. Estimated cost: $300 and up.

THE BOX SPRING

Don't bother. Most are filled with steel, and they're expensive and wasteful to ship. If you must use a box spring, choose a slat frame "foundation" instead, which serves the same purpose. A better choice is a bed frame that includes adjustable, tempered-wood slats for support under the mattress. These are available constructed of sustainable woods.

THE BEDDING

There are lots of green choices here, including organic cotton or hemp/cotton sheets and pillowcases; down pillows and comforters; and pillows stuffed with shredded natural latex or organically grown grains such as buckwheat and seed fibers like kapok and flax. When shopping, make sure the materials are certified organic, not simply "natural." Silk is also a natural fiber, but it isn't always organic (and pure silk typically requires dry cleaning). Note that satin sheets usually contain nylon or polyester thread. In addition, they're cheesy. Estimated cost: $200 per set and up.

- A single mattress can take up twenty-three cubic feet of space in a landfill and create a dangerous soft spot that can injure the frontloader drivers.

- Traditional mattresses are hard on landfill machinery, and they're composed of many different types of nonbiodegradable material.

- It's estimated that in Northern California alone, 350,000 mattresses go out of service each year.

- Mattress retailers have resisted calls for reusing old mattress parts in new mattresses, but several states (California, Oregon, and Minnesota among them) have instituted recycling programs.

- One company recycles six hundred thousand pounds a year of polyurethane foam from used mattresses; most of it is remanufactured into carpet pads.

GREEN UP FURNITURE, WALLS, AND FLOORING

Chemically treated materials—from drapes to dress shirts to recliners—are probably scattered around your bedroom. These are not only ecologically detrimental but also can make your bedroom a less relaxing and literally more toxic place. Take the following steps to green things up a bit.

REMOVE CARPETING

Standard floor carpeting is an environmental disaster: It contains glues, dyes, and chemical treatments that can off-gas, causing headaches and other discomfort. It also tends to trap dirt and dust mites, and it's difficult to clean. Instead, use small, washable, organic cotton or wool rugs.

REMOVE WALLPAPER AND GLUE

You can brighten up your bedroom without using artificial light by painting the wall opposite the windows a bright and light color that reflects sunlight. Use non-oil-based interior latex paint. If you must use wallpaper, ask for natural, nontoxic wallpaper paste (also called "non-volatile organic compound" or "non-VOC" compositions). Never, ever use vinyl wallpaper.

CHECK FURNITURE FOR CHEMICAL TREATMENTS

Any upholstered furniture that's stain resistant probably contains formaldehyde, which is said to cause insomnia. Cheap particleboard furniture is also commonly treated with this chemical. Remove these items from your bedroom.

INSTALL TOP-DOWN, BOTTOM-UP WINDOW SHADES

These models allow plenty of light into the room, but they offer privacy and the added benefit of not needing to be completely open or closed, like blinds, which helps keep the room cool in summer.

SHOP AND CARE FOR HEMP CLOTHING

Cotton is one of the world's most water- and pesticide-intensive crops. In fact, it accounts for one-quarter of all pesticides used globally and half of those used in the United States. In this country, cotton production requires more water for irrigation than either wheat or corn. And you can't eat it. Industrial hemp is easy to grow, resistant to pests and weeds, beneficial for soil, and stronger, warmer, more durable, and (in many cases) softer than cotton. There's just one small problem: It's illegal to grow it here. Clothing made from hemp grown in other countries, however, is perfectly legal. And it's a good, ecologically sound apparel choice. Use the following tips when shopping and caring for hemp.

EARTHY HUES

Natural hemp has a natural shade, similar to linen. Virtually all colored hemp clothing has been dyed with natural vegetable dyes.

WASH HOT OR COLD

Hemp clothing can be washed in the washing machine, at any temperature. Sometimes called a "machine-washable linen," hemp fabric is extremely durable. However, hand-embroidered hemp shouldn't be washed in hot water.

DRIES QUICKLY

Hemp clothing can be machine-dried, but it air-dries quickly. Air-dried hemp clothing may be stiff, like linen. Tumble dry it on a no-heat setting to soften it. You can also soften garments by hot-ironing them right out of the washer.

STYLISHLY TEXTURED

Hemp dresses should be ironed on the inside to preserve the look of the weave.

NO MOTH BALLS NEEDED

Hemp is naturally mothproof.

SOFTER BROKEN IN

Hemp typically gets softer the more it's washed. You can speed the process by washing garments in hot water, tumbling dry, then repeating.

- An acre of land planted with hemp yields two to three times more fiber than the same area planted with cotton.

- Hemp once accounted for 80 percent of the world's textiles. Its precipitous decline can be traced back to federal legislation that outlawed its use in the anti-marijuana fervor of the early twentieth century.

- Hemp contains a minuscule amount—typically 0.3–1.5 percent—of THC, the psychoactive drug found in cannabis flowers (marijuana), which contain 5–10 percent THC. However, the levels in hemp wouldn't even be enough to give you a headache.

- Betsy Ross sewed the first American flag from hemp.

CONSTRUCT A HEADLAMP

Headlamps are handy for a green bedroom: They leave your hands free to hold a book or perform other bedroom activities; they focus light exactly where you need it; they keep the room dim, which encourages falling asleep; and they use less energy than a light fixture. Throw in a few rechargeable batteries to power it and you've got a money-saving, environmentally conscious bedroom assistant. And it's a great shin saver when getting that midnight snack.

MATERIALS	$10

- ☐ Portable spotlight that includes or accepts rechargeable batteries (available at big-box or outdoor stores)
- ☐ Head-size sweatband
- ☐ Large, diaper-type safety pin
- ☐ Duct tape
- ☐ Scissors

You can purchase a headlamp from outdoor and camping stores (try www.rei.com or www.llbean.com) for $20–$50. Note that these units typically don't contain rechargeable batteries—and they may run on expensive watch-type batteries.

WARNING: Use caution when both bedmates are wearing headlamps, to avoid a nasty collision.

STEPS TO CONSTRUCT THE LAMP

1. Prepare headlamp. If necessary, charge the internal battery. If purchasing a lamp that requires batteries, select one that accepts a AA or AAA size. Avoid headlamps that accept only watch-type batteries, as these are non-rechargeable and expensive.

2. Prepare sweatband. Open the safety pin. Place the sweatband between the two prongs, then close it. The prong shouldn't actually poke through the sweatband, allowing the pin to slide freely along it.

3. Cut tape: Using the scissors, cut a 1-inch piece of tape. Feed it behind the outer side of the safety pin—the side that won't touch your forehead—with the sticky side facing out.

4. Attach the headlamp to the tape and secure it. You should now have a headlamp with a lamp that slides freely along the sweatband, allowing easy side-to-side adjustment. To raise or lower the beam, slide the front of the sweatband up or down while moving the back in the opposite direction.

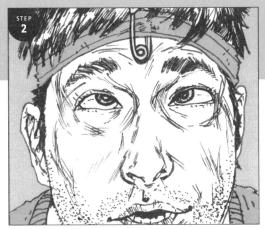

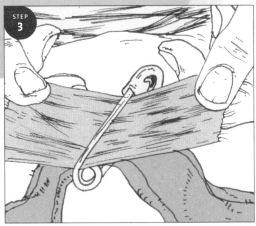

SET YOUR BODY CLOCK INSTEAD OF AN ALARM CLOCK

You can save electricity (or batteries) by eschewing an alarm clock and instead "programming" your body clock to wake you at a specific time of day. Use the tips below to prime your body and brain for regular, timely awakenings.

MONITOR DAYLIGHT EXPOSURE AND ADJUST AS NECESSARY

The body's natural circadian rhythms are controlled by internal mechanisms, but they can be modulated by daylight exposure. Make sure you're exposed to natural daylight during the day. If you work in a windowless office, get outside—especially during fall and winter, when it may be dark by the time you leave work. Regular, consistent exposure to daylight will help maintain your body's natural sleep-wake cycle.

ADJUST ROOM LIGHT

At night, your bedroom should be dark, not dim. A fully dark room cues the brain that it is time to sleep. Use an eyeshade, if available.

CHECK ROOM TEMPERATURE

At night, the brain signals the body to reduce heat production and allow more heat loss. Make sure your bed has adequate blankets to combat any chill that may wake you during the night. (The average adult's temperature reaches its minimum at five o'clock in the morning, typically about two hours before habitual waking time.)

FOLLOW A ROUTINE

While an occasional short afternoon nap shouldn't affect your natural waking time, significantly varying the hour you go to bed can. Conversely, waking up at the same time each morning will help your body and brain fall into a desirable pattern. Before you fall asleep, focus your mind on your desired waking time. Don't change your pattern on weekends.

AVOID ALCOHOL

Alcohol consumption can disrupt sleep patterns in a number of ways, including exacerbating (and even causing) sleep apnea, increasing wakefulness at night, and forcing frequent nighttime bathroom trips. These hold true even for alcohol consumed many hours before bedtime.

IF YOU CAN'T SLEEP, GET OUT OF BED

Even if it's two o'clock. Your goal is to condition your mind that your bed is for sleeping, not for being awake. You're better off sitting on the sofa and reading a book in the middle of the night than tossing and turning for hours on end.

MAKE YOUR CANDLES BURN LONGER

With the exception of sunlight, candles—especially those derived from beeswax and plant oils and not from paraffin (petroleum) or tallow (animal fat)—are the most energy-efficient means of illumination. Unfortunately, although they may be made from renewable resources, candles themselves are nonrenewable: Once they burn down, they require replacement. Use the following tips and tricks to get the most from this eco-friendly light source.

TRIM WICKS

In general, wicks should be no longer than one-quarter inch. Shorter wicks receive a steadier, more even flow of oxygen, produce less soot, and reduce the length of the flame, which melts less wax. The exception is tapers, which should produce long flames and typically have "smokeless" wicks that burn down naturally.

REFRIGERATE BEFORE USE

An hour before lighting your candles, place them in the refrigerator to increase burn time. Wrap them in plastic wrap or foil to prevent the wicks from absorbing moisture. Do not freeze them.

BURN PILLARS PROPERLY

On initial lighting, pillar candles should be burned one hour for every inch of candle diameter. This creates an even melting pool and reduces "tunneling," where only one side of the candle melts.

KEEP CANDLES OUT OF DRAFTS

Drafts make candles burn unevenly.

AVOID JARS

As they burn, jarred candles typically have less access to oxygen and thus melt unevenly and create more soot. Consider removing them from their containers.

THE SOFTER THE WAX, THE FASTER THE BURN

Although well-made soy candles may burn for a long time, less expensive ones tend to be soft and melt quickly.

MONITOR BURN TIME

In general, a candle shouldn't be burned for more than three hours before it's extinguished and the wick trimmed.

USE BEESWAX

Beeswax candles are the most eco-friendly type: They're smoke-free, nontoxic, and hypoallergenic. All candles emit small amounts of CO_2, however.

GREEN CLEANING TIPS

10 NEAT TIPS

WIPE WOOD SURFACES WITH A NATURAL WOOD SOAP

You can also make a solution of one part white vinegar to one part vegetable oil; add a few drops of lemon oil for fragrance. Mineral oil is safe for most untreated wood surfaces and is nontoxic.

DUST UNDER YOUR BED

You can use a small vacuum or a natural dust mop to reduce dust bunnies, mites, and dirt that can interfere with restful sleep.

CLEAN WINDOWS, WINDOW SCREENS, BLINDS, AND WINDOWSILLS ONCE A MONTH

Dirty windows dull the sunlight that enters the room, and dirty sills, blinds, and screens contribute to dust. Mrs. Meyer's cleaning products (www.mrsmeyers.com) are excellent eco-friendly choices here. You can also make a solution of one-quarter cup of white vinegar mixed with two cups of water. Clean the glass only when it's cool.

ELIMINATE CLUTTER DAILY

Or every two days. If you wait a week, you risk feeling overwhelmed, which can lead to cleaning paralysis. A clutter-free bedroom is a more relaxing place.

TAKE AREA RUGS OUTSIDE
Smack them with a broom or baseball bat to remove dust and dust mites.

USE A COMFORTER COVER
It's easier to wash and dry than a comforter. Wash it once a month.

AIR OUT YOUR MATTRESS MONTHLY
Exposing your mattress to sunlight for a few hours each month will reduce mold, mildew, moisture, and dust mites.

WASH PILLOWS ONCE A MONTH
Most pillows can stand hot water, but check the care instructions. Air-dry, then fluff them. If you must tumble dry, add a tennis ball to fluff them.

AIR OUT THE ROOM EVERY FEW DAYS
Nothing saps your energy like stale air.

REMOVE OLD MAGAZINES AND NEWSPAPERS, OR PLACE THEM VERTICALLY IN A RACK.
Lots of flat surfaces mean lots of places for dust to settle—dust that will blow all over the room when the papers are moved.

LOOK SAUCY IN SOY WEAR: DOS AND DON'TS

While they're not yet as popular and not quite as versatile as hemp clothing, soy-based garments are another eco-conscious alternative to cotton. (Bonus: Growing soy isn't illegal.) Overall, soy wear is easy to care for, affordable, and without the hippie stigma—and the endless marijuana jokes—attached to hemp. Still, there are several points to keep in mind when dressing in salt-of-the-earth clothes.

DO

DO BUY THEM FOR STRENGTH

Soy fiber is stronger than cotton, wool, or silk, and it's second only to polyester.

DO BUY THEM FOR MOTH RESISTANCE

Unlike silk and wool, soy fiber is resistant to moths. And unlike cotton, it's also resistant to fungus.

DO BUY THEM AS AN ECO-CONSCIOUS CHOICE

Soybean fiber is essentially made from waste: It's created from the leftover dregs of soybean oil, tofu, and soy milk production. The protein liquids are spun from the dregs and then dried, to make fiber. The remaining raw materials from this process, bean dregs, can be used as fodder or natural fertilizer. No petrochemicals are used in soy fiber production, and the clothing is biodegradable.

DO WATCH FOR FUZZING, BUT NOT PILLING

Is that a do or a don't? Anyway, soy garments will fuzz like fine cashmere but tend not to pill like wool.

DO BUY THEM FOR WARMTH

Soybean protein fiber has a consistency similar to silk, and when knitted it's similar to a blend of silk and cashmere. It's also very lightweight, is almost as warm as wool, and has better ventilation and moisture transmission than cotton, making it ideal for activewear.

DO BUY THEM FOR EASE OF CARE

Soy-based garments can be washed by hand or in the washing machine (in cold water) and air-dried. They tend not to wrinkle as much as cotton fabrics, and they don't hold creases.

DON'T WASH IN HOT WATER

Soy clothing washed in hot water may shrink. But aside from bedding, towels, and undergarments, you really don't need to wash anything in hot water anyway.

DON'T MACHINE-DRY THEM

Use a clothesline.

DON'T EXPECT THEM TO COST A LOT

In terms of price, soy wear is equivalent to similar garments made from cotton or nylon. The online retailer www.gaiam.com carries soy wear and other organically grown clothing.

Wool is also a sustainable replacement for cotton. But just because a garment is made from a sheep doesn't mean it's ecologically sound. For example, the clothing company Patagonia recently performed an "energy audit" on one of its wool shirts. The wool is sheared from sheep in New Zealand; sent to a Japanese textile factory for processing; shipped to California for sewing; packaged in Reno, Nevada; and then shipped to stores and homes. And what's behind that one shirt? Sixteen thousand miles, forty-seven pounds of carbon dioxide emissions, and eighty-nine megajoules of energy—enough to power the average U.S. home for twenty hours.

- In the 1940s, auto magnate Henry Ford was photographed wearing the first known soy suit and tie. Ford was a big proponent of soybeans, which he used to manufacture "soy plastic" panels for his company's cars.

- Soy is sometimes called a sanitary fiber, because of the antibacterial properties of soy garments.

CHAPTER 4

THE KIDS' ROOM
Organic Play

Kids are information sponges, which makes them excellent candidates for a green education. Unfortunately, they're also big energy wasters: They go through cheap plastic toys like locusts; they leave everything turned on and/or running; and they're not big on sacrifice. The good news is that the projects in this chapter are quick and easy and, most important, fun ways to keep them entertained while also teaching the benefits of conservation, from building a carbon-neutral dollhouse to making eco-forts to growing herbs with Chia Pets. Also included are a bunch of ways to save energy in their rooms at very little or zero cost. Pretty soon they'll be lecturing you on your wasteful ways. Then you'll know you've succeeded.

CONSTRUCT A CARBON-NEUTRAL DOLLHOUSE

Typical dollhouse fittings and furniture are either petroleum-based (plastic) or wood. Metals (including mined and smelted metals such as pewter, tin, silver, and brass) are also sometimes used in the fabrication of high-end, McMansion-style doll homes. (And these days, many of the interior furnishings are shipped from overseas.) Fortunately, it's easy and fun to build a dollhouse with all-natural, recycled materials found around your own house.

MATERIALS	$0

- ☐ Three or four medium-size corrugated cardboard boxes (sturdy liquor boxes work well)
- ☐ Homemade paste (see Step 1)
- ☐ Scissors or matte knife
- ☐ Old magazines
- ☐ Ruler and pencil
- ☐ Two round toothpicks, broken in half, or four pushpins
- ☐ Food coloring to make homemade paint (optional; see Step 1)

You can use empty cereal boxes as prefabricated walls.

STEPS TO CONSTRUCT THE HOUSE

1. Make the paste: Add cold water to 1/2 cup of flour and mix until it's smooth. Pour mixture into a saucepan and simmer for 5 minutes. Allow to cool for 5–10 minutes, then use it as you would store-bought paste. (You can make extra paste and turn it into dollhouse paint by adding a little extra water and a few drops of food coloring while it's on the stove. Apply it to walls with a paintbrush while it's wet.)

2. Make the roof: First, assemble supports for the roof and walls. Using the scissors or matte knife, cut four strips of cardboard, each 12 x 2 inches wide. Then cut one strip 24 x 2 inches. Score each strip down the center lengthwise, then bend it to form long, wide Vs. Set the four shorter strips aside. Next, cut two square pieces, each 12 x 24 inches. These are the two sides of the gabled roof. Hold the longer V support so the point is facing up (that is, the V is upside down) and apply paste along both long sides. Press and hold one long edge of each roof panel to the paste until it hardens. You should now have a V-shaped gabled roof.

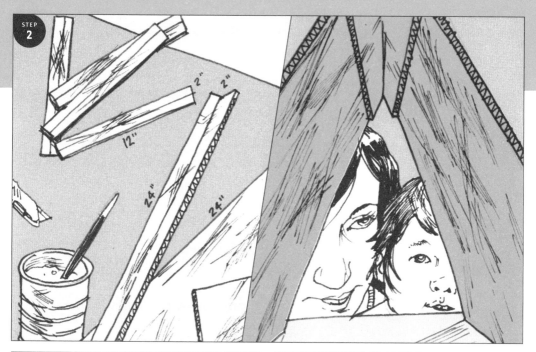

3. Make the walls: You should make four walls, with the front wall removable so you can access the interior from the front as well as the top. Cut four pieces of cardboard, two pieces 12 x 24 inches (the front and back) and two pieces 12 x 12 inches (the sides). Draw and cut out squares or rectangles for doors and windows, and paint or decorate the walls, as desired.

4. Secure walls to supports: As with the roof, apply paste to the sides of two V-shaped supports and attach the short ends of the back and two side pieces of the house. You should have a three-sided rectangle, open at the front. When this section is dry, paste the two additional supports to the open ends, leaving one side of the support without paste. Using the toothpick pieces or the pushpins, secure the front of the house to the two supports so it can be removed when necessary.

5. Make room dividers: Cut and fold cardboard pieces into L shapes to make movable interior walls. Cut patterns and images from the old magazines and paste them to the walls to make wallpaper and "paintings."

6. Place the roof on the house: You can add a chimney by cutting a section of a toilet paper roll at an angle and pasting it to the top.

You can, of course, use any existing doll furniture you have lying around for your recycled dollhouse. However, many common household items are good substitutes. Use an empty thread spool as a coffee table; small cardboard produce containers (as from raspberries or blueberries), cut in half and topped with cotton balls, as a sofa; a single cardboard egg holder attached to a straw as a floor lamp; and matchboxes, stacked and glued, as drawers.

QUICK AND EFFICIENT WAYS TO SAVE ENERGY

8 EASY TRICKS

SWITCH OUT INCANDESCENT NIGHT-LIGHTS

Use a four-watt mini-fluorescent lightbulb, or an electroluminescent night-light (which is also cool to the touch). Both save electricity. To save even more, choose a night-light with a small light meter that detects ambient light and keeps the light off when the room is illuminated by conventional lights or sunlight. Estimated cost: $5 each.

INSTALL DOOR-SWITCHED CLOSET LIGHTS

Kids tend to turn closet lights on and forget them. Install a push button switch that turns the light off when the door is closed. However, since kids also tend to leave doors open, place lights in timed fixtures that turn off after five minutes. Estimated cost: It varies based on the fixture type, but about $25 each.

SWAP CURTAINS

Light-colored, loose-weave curtains let in plenty of light during the day. They also let moonlight filter in—and since most kids don't want a black room at night anyway, it's win-win. Use shades to keep the room cool on hot summer days. Estimated cost: $25–$50 per window.

USE BRIGHT COLORS

Bright paint reflects sunlight, and kids are partial to bold colors anyway. Consider a brightly painted mural instead of one solid color. Estimated cost: $15 per gallon of paint.

USE CFL BULBS, BUT WISELY

Compact fluorescent lightbulbs save electricity and are appropriate for permanent fixtures in the kids' room. However, because they contain small amounts of mercury and have special cleanup requirements when shattered, they shouldn't be used in standing or tabletop fixtures that can topple. (Dust the bulbs regularly, too; a thick coating of dust can reduce the light output by half.) Estimated cost: $5 each.

PUT VIDEO GAME CONSOLES ON A POWER STRIP

Teach the kids to turn the strip off every night, or use a "smart strip" (see Make Your Audio/Video Equipment More Eco-Friendly, page 46).

CHECK COMPUTERS EACH NIGHT

Kids tend to be blissfully unaware that their computers and monitors use lots of energy (one hundred watts at times). And they also tend to leave the devices on all the time, lest they miss a crucial instant message. Make sure both PC and monitor are set to sleep/standby/hibernate after ten minutes of inactivity. Ask your kids to show you where the setting is.

CHECK FLOOR VENTS AND HEATING REGISTERS REGULARLY

Kids pile stuff everywhere—including on top of floor vents, which blocks airflow. Make sure the vents and radiators are unobstructed, to keep rooms cooled and heated efficiently.

BUILD AN ECO-FORT

It's probably safe to assume your kids won't be building forts with coal-burning stoves and central air. Still, it's never too early to reinforce the benefits of being ecologically aware. Below are tips and tricks to get the youngest conservationists in the family thinking about how to conserve energy around your own house.

GREEN TREE HOUSE

If you live in the suburbs, this is probably the most commonly requested type of fort. However, traditional tree house construction methods not only use new lumber but also tend to damage the tree that holds the fort. Tree-safe tree houses use lashing (that is, rope) with special knotting to hold the platform in place without damaging the tree. If you cannot lash the platform, make sure to use galvanized or stainless steel lag bolts; nongalvanized bolts will rust and encourage rot. Visit building sites (make sure to get permission first) and ask for damaged or scrap wood, but avoid highly knotted wood as it's not as structurally sound. Pressure-treated wood may last longer, but it's not eco-friendly, and you should avoid breathing in any sawdust. Don't build your tree house too high: For small kids, five to six feet off the ground will seem plenty high once they're up there. And build only on a large, mature tree.

RECYCLED BOX FORT

Large appliance boxes make excellent forts, and since many municipalities don't recycle cardboard, you'll be reducing your waste stream in the process. Refrigerator boxes, of course, are ideal for forts—but most of us don't buy refrigerators on a regular basis. Instead, save packing boxes, diaper boxes, and boxes from deliveries until you have a large supply, then cut them open with a matte knife to create cardboard sheets. Join the sheets together with masking tape to make a large fort. If the boxes won't stand on their own, suspend a length of rope about four feet off the ground between two heavy objects and use it to build a cardboard lean-to or A-frame fort.

ORGANIC SHEET AND PILLOW FORT

Kids love to hide and play under sheets stretched across stacks of pillows. To reinforce a green message, have the children draw a sign labeling the fort "organic" and, during construction, use only natural fibers grown and manufactured without pesticides or herbicides. Inside the fort, serve snacks of organic carrots, organic juices, and cookies made from organic ingredients.

> WARNING: A sudden release of methane by one of its occupants may cause an immediate evacuation of the fort.

RAIN-CATCHER UMBRELLA FORT

In less than five minutes, you and the kids can construct an outdoor fort that offers shelter *and* collects rainwater for later use. First, open four large umbrellas (big, golf-type umbrellas work best). Place them on the ground so their handles touch and their edges overlap to form a domed room. Leave a small space as a door. Next, tie or rubber-band the handles together (this allows the fort to be moved easily). Crawl into the fort. From inside, position five or six small plastic or ceramic bowls so they sit directly under the points where the umbrellas touch the ground. As rain hits the umbrellas, the water will travel down the nylon and land in the bowls, where it can be used to water plants.

MAKE A CHIA PET HERB GARDEN

Kids love Chia Pets because they're fun to watch as the chia seeds—*Salvia hispanica*, actually a member of the mint family—sprout and grow, quickly covering the pet with a lush coat of green "fur." Nutritionally, you'd probably be better off eating the seeds than growing the herb, though it, too, is edible. Replacing the chia seeds with a more versatile herb will be more of a benefit in the kitchen—and can save you money.

MATERIALS	$12

- ☐ Chia Pet kit (available online at drugstore.com as well as at some retail drugstores and big-box retailers such as Target)
- ☐ Replacement herb seeds (consider chives, cilantro, dill, marjoram, wheatgrass, or basil)
- ☐ Water
- ☐ Spray bottle

Joseph Enterprises, the maker of Chia Pets—and, incidentally, the Clapper—sells a product called Chia Herb Garden. But it's nothing more than seeds, soil, and some tiny pots. And where's the fun in that?

STEPS TO GROW THE GARDEN

1. Prepare seeds. Open the Chia Pet kit and replace the chia seeds with your herb choice, or just mix them together. Moisten the seeds according to seed pack instructions. Let them stand for 24 hours.

2. Soak the Chia planter in water for 24 hours. Remove it and place on the kit's drip tray.

3. Spread the moistened seeds on the Chia Pet.

4. Place the Chia Pet in a location with indirect sunlight. Windowsills with direct light may cause the seeds to become dry.

5. Fill the Chia Pet regularly with water, empty the drip tray as it fills, and mist the seeds using the spray bottle. Don't let the seeds become dry or they'll die.

6. To hasten sprouting, cover the Chia Pet with a plastic bag—don't let it touch the seeds—to create a humid, greenhouse-like environment. The seeds should sprout within five days. Remove the bag after they sprout.

7. Clip herbs regularly. Stem herbs such as cilantro will tend to flop over as they grow, so cut them regularly to maintain the Chia's lush "fur coat" appearance.

8. Repeat Steps 1–7 with additional Chia Pets and different herbs. The ceramic Chia Pet planter itself is infinitely reusable; so don't despair if your herbs don't succeed. Remove the dead seeds and start again.

- Chia seeds are high in fiber, rich in antioxidants, and contain very high levels of omega-3 fatty acids, also found in salmon and other oily fish. Dr. Andrew Weil, the best-selling author and health guru, recommends sprinkling chia seeds on salads for a healthy dose of omega-3.

- Chia seeds are safe to eat raw—the way they're eaten in Mexico, where they're cultivated—but can also be ground into pinole, a type of flour used by Aztecs and American Indians in cooking.

- The Aztecs were said to use chia medicinally, to relieve joint pain and skin conditions.

- In Mexico, you can buy a *chia fresca*, a drink made by combining two teaspoons of chia seeds, ten ounces of water, sugar, and lime or lemon juice.

ECO-SMART PLAY FOR A DARK ROOM

5 FUN GAMES

When the sun goes down, the kids aren't always (or, perhaps, ever) ready to turn in. Instead of turning on the lights and the energy-hungry flat-screen television, consider games that take advantage of the dark. Such games may also make children more comfortable in their beds at night, when shadows tend to look like scary, looming strangers. (These activities can also be useful during power outages.)

FLASHLIGHT SCAVENGER HUNT

Kids *love* to play with flashlights. Hide some toys or treats in plain sight, then turn the lights off. Give each child his or her own flashlight and let them search for the "hidden" objects. Use rechargeable batteries.

GUESS THE FOOD

Out of the children's sight, place the following foods in separate bowls: cooked spaghetti (in cold water), gelatin, cooked or frozen peas, grapes, dried lentils, and bread crumbs. Turn the lights off. Let the kids place their hands in the bowls and try to guess what they're touching. Keep a towel handy.

"CAMPING"

Pitch a small tent in a darkened room. Give the kids a rechargeable battery-powered lantern and let them sleep in sleeping bags. Tell ghost stories. Avoid campfires.

SHADOW PUPPETS

This age-old game requires nothing more than your hands, a flashlight, and a very dark room. Most of us know how to make simple animals like a rabbit, dove, or dog. But how about a turtle? Or an old man? Or particular *breeds* of dog? The Web site http://haha.nu/creative/how-to-make-shadows-on-the-wall/ has easy-to-follow illustrations to make lots of shadow puppets.

GLOW-IN-THE-DARK ANYTHING

Rare is the kid who isn't fascinated by *anything* that glows in the dark. Even clocks and watches. Some toys, however, especially bracelets, necklaces, and glow sticks, are chemical-based and lose their glow properties quickly once activated. Instead, consider glow-in-the-dark stickers (stars and planets, dinosaurs) and luminescent versions of popular games, including, tops, puzzles, tic-tac-toe, and even pin-the-tail-on-the-donkey.

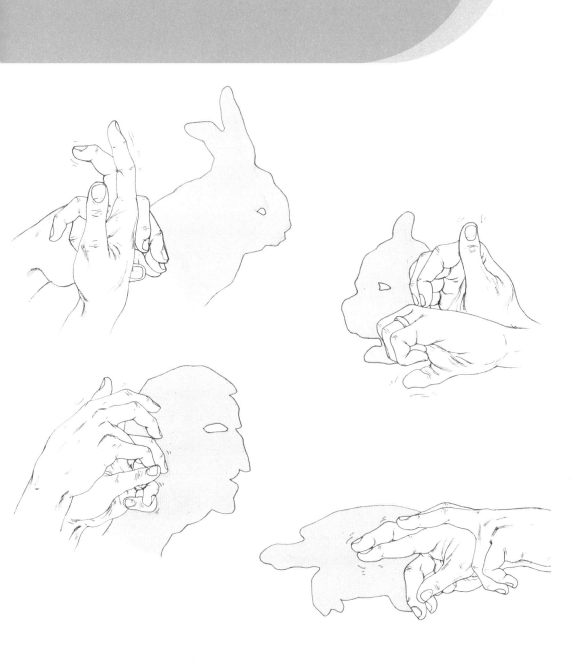

CHAPTER 5

THE BATHROOM
Wastewater Treatment

Just turn the faucet and the water pours out. Flush the toilet or drain the tub and all the water disappears. Like magic! Not exactly. We spend hundreds of billions of dollars each year, in utility bills and taxes, to make water safe for drinking and to treat our wastewater. We pay billions more for unnecessary bottled water and yet we waste billions of gallons by letting the water run and by using inefficient appliances. In this chapter, you'll learn how to use water—and the appliances that require water—much more efficiently, from shaving to bathing to flushing. You'll also learn how to make your electric toothbrush more efficient and how to choose the greenest toilet paper. You'll even learn how to take a warm shower without paying a cent for hot water. And how to survive a "navy shower."

MAKE A TOILET SINK

When it comes to toilets, there are a number of ways to save water. You can—and really *should*, honestly—switch to a low-flow model; these are relatively cheap and available at home-improvement stores. You can also lower the water level (the "fill line") inside the tank. Or you can use the age-old "brick-in-the-tank" trick of displacing some of the water volume. (This last method works, but there's a better alternative; see Carbon Counter, on the next page) But the best method is to fill the tank with gray water that would otherwise be wasted down the drain. And that means building a toilet sink.

MATERIALS	$40

- ☐ Small plastic washbasin, with drain and lip, approximately 7 inches in diameter, available at most home-improvement stores. (It should be no wider than your toilet tank lid, typically 7 1/2 inches wide.)
- ☐ Sheet of plywood or similar scrap wood
- ☐ Jigsaw
- ☐ Keyhole saw
- ☐ Drill
- ☐ Water jug
- ☐ Grease pencil

STEPS TO MAKE THE SINK

1. Remove the toilet tank lid. Place it on the plywood.

2. Using the grease pencil, trace around the tank lid, then remove it.

3. Cut out the traced section of the plywood, using the jigsaw.

4. Again using the grease pencil, color the inner edge of the washbasin's lip, coating it completely. Turn the washbasin upside down and press it against the wood. The pencil should transfer to the wood, giving you a perfect circle to cut.

5. Drill a hole, widen it with the keyhole saw, then cut out the circle, using the jigsaw.

6. Insert the basin into the plywood up to the lip. Place the plywood on top of the tank. Make sure the basin doesn't interfere with the toilet handle or tank components.

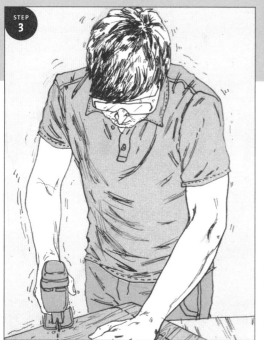

You can purchase a premade toilet sink for about $100 from www.gaiam.com and other retailers. Naturally, this device is more expensive than a do-it-yourself model, but it has the advantage of running water, obviating the need for a water jug. A company called WaterSaver Technologies sells the AQUS Water Saving Device, which operates under the same basic principle but connects the toilet directly to the sink and filters and disinfects water before it enters the tank—so you can still use the sink for shaving, toothbrushing, and so on. It costs about $200 at www.watersavertech.com.

7. Turn off the water supply to the toilet.

8. For hand washing, simply use water from the jug and natural liquid soap to clean your hands over the toilet top basin. The wastewater will fill the tank and be used whenever you flush. You may need to adjust the amount of water you use to make sure there's enough in the tank to flush the toilet fully.

- Americans flush twelve trillion gallons of freshwater down the toilet each year.

- Leaky U.S. toilets waste five trillion gallons of water each year. A constantly running toilet usually means the ball and flapper aren't making a tight seal with the rubber O-ring at the bottom of the tank and should be replaced.

- The brick-in-the-tank trick does save water, but experts don't recommend it because minerals leaching from the brick can foul the mechanism. Try a small plastic container filled with sand or pebbles instead.

- Make sure to use a natural soap, such as Castile (see Green Bits, page 100), when using your toilet sink. Chemical agents may degrade the flushing mechanism.

- Don't use your toilet sink to, say, wash the dishes. Only soap and water should enter the toilet tank, or you risk fouling the mechanism.

- Despite rumors to the contrary, toilet tank water is not safe to drink, ever, because bacteria may enter the tank through a leaky O-ring or loose ball and flapper.

TAKE A NAVY SHOWER

The navy shower (or "eye-opener") is a refreshing way to start the day and save buckets of water at the same time. A brisk rinse off is also a good time-saver: You won't want to linger. It also saves hot water, which requires energy to heat. (On very cold mornings, use warm water to reduce the chance of hypothermia.)

MATERIALS	$5

- ☐ Washcloth
- ☐ Medium-size (1–2 gallon) bucket or large bowl
- ☐ Liquid Castile soap (see "Build a Plunger Washing Machine," page 100).

Cotton is a chemically intensive crop. Plush cotton bath towels—including some that are labeled "organic" or "all natural"—are typically grown in chemically treated soil. Most towels are also chemically treated during manufacture to make them softer. If you must use a towel, use a superabsorbent "body chamois" type of travel towel. It's just as effective as a plush cotton towel, but it's smaller and dries in minutes, reducing mildew and the need for washing. Wet it slightly and snap it a few times before using to remove stiffness.

STEPS TO TAKE A SHOWER

1. Get in the shower or tub.

2. Turn the water on cold and fill the bucket. Turn water off.

3. Dip the washcloth in the bucket.

4. Saturate your body with the washcloth, redip the cloth, then squeeze water onto your hair.

5. Squeeze out a palmful of the Castile soap.

6. Rub hands together vigorously to create a lather. Spread the soap on your body and hair.

7. Dip the washcloth in the bucket.

8. Rub washcloth over your body to remove the soap. Wring out the washcloth. Redip if necessary.

9. Dump the remaining water in the bucket over your head to remove soap. Don't refill the bucket unless the water is too soapy.

10. Wick moisture from your body using hands or a homemade body squeegee (see Make a Body Squeegee, page 90).

11. Get out of the shower and do thirty jumping jacks to air-dry.

BUILD AN OUTDOOR SOLAR SHOWER

There's nothing quite like an outdoor shower—in the summer, anyway. Solar showers have been a staple of (clean) campers forever, but they're perfect for a green home, too—provided you have the necessary space, privacy, and sunlight requirements. And you don't mind waiting for the water to heat up. They save energy, of course, but solar showers also save water: You'll learn to shower using less of it.

MATERIALS	$10

- ☐ Large (30-gallon) contractor-type garbage bag, black only
- ☐ Plastic shower nozzle with cutoff valve and attached flexible tubing (available at home supply stores)
- ☐ Band clamp
- ☐ Sturdy rope
- ☐ Scissors
- ☐ Screwdriver
- ☐ Clear packing tape (optional)
- ☐ Small dowel (optional)

You can purchase a ready-made solar shower from camping stores for about $20.

WARNING: Use only natural soap with this shower.

STEPS TO BUILD THE SHOWER

1. Using the scissors, cut a 1-inch section off one corner of the bottom of the garbage bag.

2. Thread about 2 inches of the open end of the tubing through the hole.

3. Pinch the bag around the tube, then place the band clamp around the bag and tube. Tighten with the screwdriver. Put some water in the bag and test it for leaks at the connection. If the bag leaks, remove the clamp, secure the bag to the tube using packing tape, then reattach clamp.

4. Fill the bag with about 5 gallons of cool water.

5. Roll down the top of the bag, making sure that there's some air above the water but the bag isn't full of air. Gather the open end of the bag together and tie a knot, as you would before throwing out a bag of trash. (To help you reopen the knot later, consider placing the dowel in the center of the knot before tying it.)

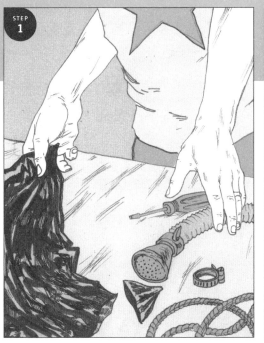

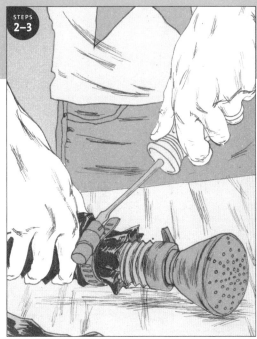

A five-minute shower under a water-saving showerhead still uses 10–20 gallons.

6. Place the rope just under the knot and tie a sturdy square knot or slipknot. Remember, the bag will be heavy—5 gallons equals about 41 pounds—so make sure the rope won't slip and the bag is securely tied. You'll need to open the bag to refill it, so a slipknot is probably the best choice.

7. Run the rope over a sturdy tree branch— or connect it to a secure bolt or hook—at a height of 7–8 feet. (If using a bolt or hook, see Green Bits, right.)

8. Let the shower sit in the sun for 2–3 hours. The water should reach the approximate air temperature, but it may be slightly warmer.

9. Shower. Use the cutoff valve when soaping your body, to save water. Ideally, the shower will be positioned over an outside drain. If not, consider covering the surrounding ground with sand and garden pebbles. Don't shower on your lawn.

- The trick to an effective solar shower is having as much of the water bag as possible exposed to the sun. Thus, a bag hanging from a bolt or hook mounted to the side of your house isn't ideal in terms of water heating. If an appropriate tree isn't available—or the only one you have is too exposed—consider hanging the water bag from a post.

- Because it takes less energy to heat air than water, the key to this home-built solar shower is trapping some air in the bag, on top of the water. As the air is heated, it will heat the water below it. Of course, too much air will make the bag unwieldy.

- Contractor bags are very sturdy. However, they're not puncture-proof. Consider using two bags if you're nervous about leaks.

MAKE A BODY SQUEEGEE

Let's just admit it. If we own a machine dryer, most of us will never choose to hang our towels on the line to dry them. Why? Because air-drying makes them about as stiff as cardboard. What's an eco-conscious bather to do? Simple. Use a body squeegee. It's cheap, quick, and lasts for years, and you can also use it to wash your windows.

MATERIALS	$4

- ☐ Hand-held plastic squeegee, available at auto parts stores
- ☐ Suction cup hook (optional, for storage)

STEPS TO MAKE THE SQUEEGEE

1. Take a (short) normal shower, or a navy shower (see page 85).

2. Turn the water off.

3. Spread apart the thumb and forefinger of your dominant hand. Place the curved section of the hand against your appendages. Using a fast, steady motion, move your hand down to wick excess moisture away. Your skin should now be damp but not soaking wet.

4. Hold the squeegee in your dominant hand. Press the edge of the rubber blade against a section of damp skin and carefully pull the squeegee down and away, as you would on a window. Any remaining water should be pushed by the blade down your body and then down the drain. Repeat with your non-dominant hand.

You can buy a purpose-built body squeegee (the Bodyflik) for about $12 at www.bodyflik.com. But it won't work on your windows.

- When exposed to air, natural rubber becomes dry and brittle over time. Keep the squeegee out of direct sunlight to slow the process.

- Although it's not a natural product, a squeegee with a silicone rubber blade, if available, may be more comfortable and durable.

- If you use a towel, drape it over the top edge of a door rather than folding it and placing it on a towel bar. It'll dry faster, reducing mildew buildup. Even better, place it on a drying rack.

5. Hang the squeegee on the hook when finished. If necessary, use a body chamois (travel towel) to dry your hair and back, or allow them to air-dry.

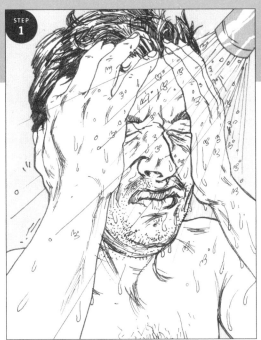

STEP 1

STEP 3

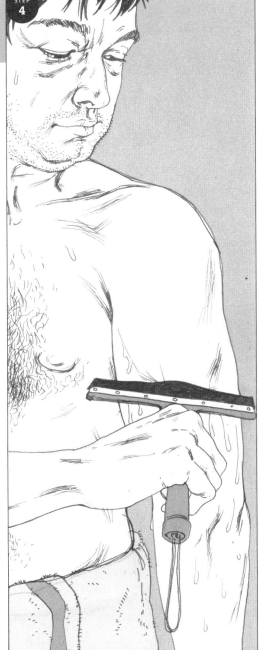

STEP 4

MAKE YOUR ELECTRIC TOOTHBRUSH MORE EFFICIENT

It's unavoidable: Brushing your teeth is no longer guilt-free. Forget about water usage; electric toothbrushes are among the numerous household gadgets that use electricity even when they're "off" (see "Carbon Counter," page 51, for a list). One study has calculated that a single electric toothbrush accounts for forty-eight grams of carbon emissions per day. Worse, the jury (of dentists) seems to split on whether or not they're more effective than brushing with a Stone Age "manual" toothbrush. Nevertheless, if you own one, there are a few tricks that will make it more efficient.

USE RECHARGEABLES

Even the toothpaste companies have jumped on the electric brush bandwagon. But these cheap (often less than $10) models almost always use standard disposable batteries. If you own one of these, at least swap out the standard AAs for a pair of rechargeables.

MONITOR THE "CHARGED" INDICATOR LIGHT

High-quality electric toothbrushes typically have an LED that indicates when the brush is charging and when it's fully charged. When the unit's battery is charged, remove it from the stand—and keep it off. Trickle charging isn't necessary.

UNPLUG THE STAND

As noted above, most toothbrush chargers use electricity even when they're not actively charging the brush. Unplug the stand when it's not in use.

USE THE BRUSH UNTIL IT LOSES ITS CHARGE

Many new electric brushes can operate for a week between charges with no degradation in rotational power. When the battery gets low—you'll know by the sound—recharge it overnight.

USE THE LOW-POWER SETTING

Some models include two rotational settings for the bristles: normal and slower. The slower setting uses less power. Try brushing on this setting.

MONITOR THE BRUSH HEAD

Naturally, electric toothbrush makers want you to purchase replacement heads (bristles) as frequently as possible. Of course, these used plastic heads contribute to your nonbiodegradable waste stream. If the bristle head holds its shape—the individual bristles are still firm and not sagging or bent—replacement is unnecessary. Soak the head in hydrogen peroxide once a week to kill bacteria.

SELECT THE GREENEST TOILET PAPER

Choosing toilet tissue used to be as simple as "soft or Scott?" Alas, for the eco-conscious user those days are gone. There's now a wealth of "green" products, each brand touting attributes such as "chemical-free," "dye-free," and "recycled." Below are some tips.

KNOW YOUR CHLORINE ACRONYMS

You may see a label that indicates the toilet tissue is "elemental chlorine free," or "ECF." Sounds great, right? Chlorine = dioxin = toxic poison = bad. Thus, ECF = no chlorine = good, right? Not exactly. ECF means that while no pure (in other words, "elemental") chlorine was used in the paper's manufacture (typically for bleaching), chlorine derivatives probably were. Instead, choose paper that's "processed chlorine free," or "PCF." This means no chlorine or chlorine derivatives, period.

KNOW RECYCLING PERCENTAGES

Today, there's probably no term more overused and misunderstood than "recycled." But there's recycled, and then there's *recycled*. The key here is "post-consumer waste," or "PCW." This means a product is made from a material that was actually out in the world, used, and *then* recycled—not simply something that was cast off from some manufacturing process. While there is, of course, value in any recycling effort, post-consumer recycling tends to reduce the overall waste stream more than other types. Look for toilet paper with the highest percentage of pulp made of PCW (typically, 80 percent).

LEARN ABOUT BLEACH

Toilet paper that's stark white has been bleached. Naturally, you can—and should, if you must—purchase paper products bleached with peroxide and not chlorine or another toxic agent. But do you really *need* white toilet paper, considering what you're using it for and where it's going? Brown toilet paper (made by Seventh Generation and other companies) is unbleached, and it feels the same. Bleaching doesn't soften toilet paper.

KNOW ROLLS, PLIES, AND SHEETS

Toilet paper is available in a number of configurations: "single ply" (one layer of paper), "double ply" (two layers), "double roll" (twice as many little squares per roll), and mind-numbing combinations such as "double-ply-triple-roll" and so forth. Typically, though, most users pull out about the same number of sheets each time. Thus, price being equal, you're better off getting more sheets per roll than additional plies. Got all that?

- The average American consumes seven hundred pounds of paper —including seventy roll of toilet paper—each year.

- Due to cost increases in commodity prices, many manufacturers have reduced the size or quantity of their products but kept prices the same.

- Single-ply toilet paper is easier on septic and municipal sewage systems than fancy triple-ply-quilted tissue.

SHAVE USING LESS WATER

You can actually shave using no water at all—with an electric razor. And, in fact, for "maintenance" shaves a rechargeable electric shaver is a good choice. But after you go two days without shaving, only two choices remain: grow a beard, or shave with a traditional razor blade. Take the following steps to reduce your water consumption.

MATERIALS	$0, assuming necessary materials are on hand

- ☐ Razor
- ☐ Natural shaving cream
- ☐ Water jug
- ☐ Sink with stopper or closable drain
- ☐ Toothpick (optional)

- The average shave consumes two to ten gallons of water, depending on how long and how fast the water runs.

- Most men shave using a medium-volume stream of running water. The problem is that most of the water isn't used: It just goes down the drain. If you find that a running stream of water clears razor clogs more effectively than the method described make sure to turn the water on only when clearing the razor head.

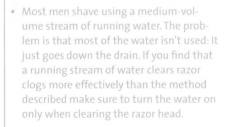

STEPS TO SHAVE WITH LESS WATER

1. Place the stopper in the sink, or shut the drain.

2. Place the water jug under the faucet. Turn the hot water on.

3. Hold the jug under the faucet to capture the cool water that emerges. When the water turns warm, remove the jug.

4. Allow the sink to fill with about 2 inches of water (about half a gallon). Turn water off.

5. Place your hand in the water jug. Pat some water onto your face to wet it, then apply shaving cream.

6. Begin shaving.

7. The blades become less effective as they get clogged with shaving cream and bristles. To clear clogs, submerge the head of the razor under the hot water in the sink and tap it vigorously against the sides until clogs are dislodged. Or use the toothpick.

8. Repeat Steps 6–7 until shaving is complete.

9. Place your hand in the jug again, splash water on your face to remove any remaining shaving cream, then air-dry or use a small towel.

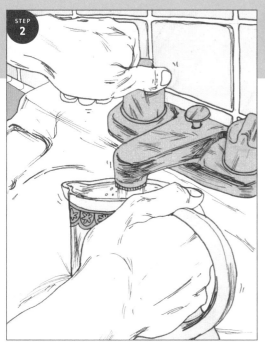

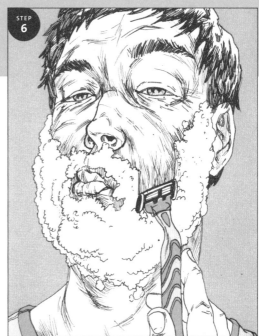

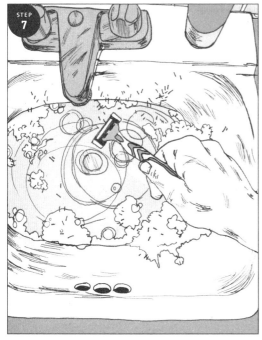

10. Drain sink. Splash some water from the jug into the sink to remove any bristles that are stuck to the sides. If any water remains in the jug, you can use it the following day; use it for hand washing and toothbrushing, or water plants with it.

Note: This method is also effective for shaving legs, and it's far more preferable than letting the water run in the shower as you shave them.

- Make sure your faucet doesn't drip. Even a single, low-volume drip adds up: Ten drips per minute equals about 350 gallons a year, or the equivalent of a week's worth of baths or two to three weeks of showers.

- You can save even more water—and the energy needed to heat it—by filling up a large glass or ceramic bowl and heating it in the microwave. (Microwaves are more energy efficient than hot water heaters.)

- If each of the sixty-eight million men in the United States who shave with a blade and razor saved one gallon of hot water per shave, the annual national savings would be 19.6 *billion* gallons of water—and about $300 million in utility costs to heat it.

- Want to save even *more* water? Consider installing a pedal-controlled sink—or convert your existing one for a few hundred dollars. Studies show that pedal sinks save thousands of gallons of water per household per year.

- Which is more eco-friendly, an electric shaver or disposable razor blades? There's no easy answer. Over time, disposable blades (and, worse, disposable plastic razors) are clearly more expensive than an electric shaver—especially in this age of umpteen-blade razor heads that cost more than a dollar a piece. Most new electric razors are fairly energy efficient and hold a charge for a week. Of course, eventually an electric razor will break down and enter the waste stream. Still, disposable razors and blades don't last very long, they're made from pollution-intensive metals and plastics, and their massive sales volume requires transportation resources. The best choice? Probably a straight razor you can sharpen yourself.

- Calculate your family's water consumption at www.nwf.org/water/watercalculator.cfm.

GREEN COSMETICS: THE GOOD, THE BAD, AND THE UGLY

You've probably heard dire warnings about the dangers of regular old "non-green" cosmetics: They *are* filled with dangerous chemicals, and they probably cause cancer. While it's true that most big-name cosmetics are filled with chemicals, it's still debated whether these chemicals pose health risks.

WHAT ARE "PARABENS"?

The cancer charges typically center around products containing parabens, usually listed as methylparaben, ethylparaben, propylparaben, and butylparaben. These chemicals are added—in small quantities and often in combination—to countless cosmetics, including lotions; shampoos, conditioners, and styling gels; sun screens; and shaving creams. They are used to retard the growth of microorganisms and prolong shelf life. Most green cosmetics eschew parabens, replacing them with natural plant extracts and herbs.

ARE THEY REALLY DANGEROUS?

In 2004, a study detected the presence of parabens in breast tumors, which spurred a flood of rumors that parabens "caused" cancer. But don't clear out the medicine cabinet quite yet.

The Food and Drug Administration is not authorized to approve ingredients in cosmetics, with a few minor exceptions. However, the Cosmetic Ingredient Review (a trade group supported by the FDA and led by a panel of medical experts) conducted a study of parabens in 1984. The study found (and a subsequent 2005 study reiterated) that parabens are safe for use in cosmetics at levels up to 25 percent; typically, parabens are used at levels ranging from 0.01 to 0.3 percent. And their safe use over many years

has convinced the FDA that parabens are not a health danger. More to the point, The American Cancer Society says that "studies have not shown any direct link between parabens and breast cancer risk."

WHY BUY GREEN?

Discounting their lack of parabens, there are other reasons to choose green cosmetics. First, they typically do not include petroleum-based chemicals, metals, or artificial dyes and fragrances. (You won't find natural deodorant with aluminum.) Second, they are not tested on animals. Third, their packaging is typically more recyclable than that used for their non-green counterparts.

Of course, green products generally cost more. This is often due to economies of scale: companies making products in smaller batches pay more when they source their ingredients. And green products are not perfect. Some natural paraben substitutes (grapefruit seed extract, for one) have themselves fallen under clouds of suspicion as to their efficacy. (Remember: "natural" does not equal "safe.") And the use of these ingredients in cosmetics is also fairly new, so their long-term heath consequences are unknown.

In the end, buying green cosmetics still makes sense. But you're probably more likely to get cancer from a source other than parabens.

CHAPTER 6

THE LAUNDRY ROOM
Clean and Green

After your heating and cooling systems, the equipment in your laundry room is the least green in your house, requiring thousands of gallons of water and massive amounts of energy—not to mention nasty things such as detergent and bleach—each year. Hand-washing your clothing helps, but it's not practical for all garments, and there's the convenience factor—or lack of it. So instead of suggesting that you never wash anything again, this chapter's projects will show you how to wash better, how to dry better (and faster, and with lower cost), and how to green-up necessary laundering evils such as—cringe—dry cleaning. Plus you'll learn about Castile soap. Woo hoo, green party in the laundry room!

BUILD A PLUNGER WASHING MACHINE

All powered clothes washers work on the same basic principle: A surfactant (detergent) is agitated in water and then forced through the wet material, separating dirt particles from it. The dirty water is then drained, and the clothes are rinsed and spun until damp. Hand-plunged washers do the same thing, using less soap and less water, with zero emissions. And churning your laundry burns calories.

MATERIALS	$20

- ☐ Wood-handled toilet plunger
- ☐ One 13–15 gallon plastic container with tight-fitting lid
- ☐ Matte knife or drill with 1/2-inch bit
- ☐ Natural laundry detergent
- ☐ Cold water
- ☐ Dirty clothes

STEPS TO BUILD THE WASHER

1. Buy a new plunger. Don't use a plunger that has plunged a toilet.

2. Cut or drill a hole, 3/4 inch in diameter, in the center of the container lid, to accept the plunger handle.

3. Thread the handle up through the hole in the lid.

4. Pour approximately 1/4 cup of environmentally friendly laundry detergent (or Castile soap; see Green Bits, above) into the bottom of the container.

- Liquid Castile soap (aka "Seafarer's soap") is a multipurpose detergent derived from various vegetable oils, not rendered animal fat. It's a safe, effective, and environmentally neutral cleaner for skin, hair, clothes, and most surfaces. The soap is said to have been invented in the Kingdom of Castile, on the Iberian Peninsula, in the seventeenth century. Castile soap is typically sold in plastic bottles that are 100 percent post-consumer recycled, and it is available in most well-stocked supermarkets and natural food stores.

- Another alternative is Wonder Wash, made by All Terrain (www.allterrainco.com). It can be used to wash anything, including hair and skin.

5. Add about 5 gallons of cold water. (Use warm water for heavily soiled clothing.) Agitate the water for 10 seconds with your hand.

6. Add the soiled clothes until the water rises to approximately the three-quarter line (no more than 5 pounds of clothing).

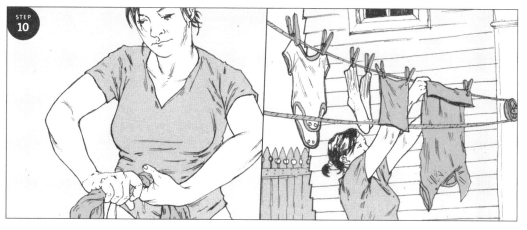

7. Place the plunger into the container, with the handle protruding from the lid. Secure lid.

8. Begin plunging. Plunge vigorously for 10 minutes. For delicate loads, this can be done with one hand while you accomplish other tasks.

9. Remove the wet clothes and place them in the sink; empty dirty water from the plunge washer; add 5 gallons of clean, cold water; replace the clothes; and repeat Steps 7–8. This is the rinse cycle.

10. To dry the clothes, wring them out or roll them in towels, then place them on a line. Very stiff clothing may be softened using an iron on its lowest (most energy-efficient) setting.

- The average American family uses a whopping sixteen thousand gallons of water each year to wash their clothes; only toilets use more.

- Front-loading, Energy Star–compliant washers are much more efficient than standard top-loading units: about 40 percent more water and energy efficient. Still, a typical load of laundry uses a minimum of fifteen gallons of water, even in an efficient machine.

- Anything that can go into the washing machine can be hand- or plunge-washed.

- One new (or actually old) technology now in favor is steam, which manufacturers are touting as a more efficient way to clean and dry clothes. (Steam dryers can even sterilize your clothes, just in case you're performing surgery right after dressing.) These new washers and dryers cost more, and the jury's still out on their overall efficiency: In some units, you can steam-dry only four articles of clothing at a time, requiring more loads and reducing any potential energy savings.

CLEAN YOUR DRYER'S EXHAUST TUBE

The efficiency of your dryer—the amount of time and energy it takes to dry a load of laundry—is affected by how clean its exhaust tube is. A lint-filled exhaust may slow drying time by 30 percent. It's also a fire hazard, since dryer lint is highly combustible.

MATERIALS	$0, assuming necessary materials are on hand

- ☐ Vacuum
- ☐ Screwdriver
- ☐ Pliers (if necessary)
- ☐ Garbage bag and masking tape (optional; see below)

STEPS TO CLEAN THE TUBE

1. Move the dryer as necessary to access the back panel. Because of its weight, the easiest method is to wiggle the unit back and forth while pulling it toward you. It should slide forward on its plastic feet. Take extra care when moving a stacked washer/dryer combo.

2. Examine the back panel. Typically, the exhaust will be a flexible tube connected to the dryer at one end and vented to the outside at the other.

3. Examine the connection to dryer. The tube should be secured to a metal plate that is attached to the dryer with four screws. Using the screwdriver, unscrew the plate.

You can hire a professional to clean your dryer vent for you. This service uses highly compressed air to blow the lint out of the dryer vent, and it typically costs about $75.

- After the refrigerator, the clothes dryer is typically the most expensive household appliance to operate, on average, with an annual cost of about $85 and a lifetime cost of about $1,500 (depending, of course, on utility rates).

- Line-drying clothes is a zero-emissions solution, though clotheslines are prohibited by zoning restrictions—and, sadly, condo boards and homeowners associations—in many places. Indoor drying racks, however, are still legal.

- The Hills Hoist, a purpose-built, umbrella-type clothesline, is extremely popular in Australia, where it's been in use for decades. Its manufacturer claims it can save users 5–10 percent on their utility bills. Visit http://www.hills.com.au for details.

4. Remove lint: Insert the vacuum's longest attachment into the loose end of the tube and vacuum out the lint. If possible, compress the tubing to reach the end. If you cannot reach the lint at the far end of the tube, continue to Step 5. Otherwise, resecure the vent tube to the dryer. Make sure it isn't coiled.

5. Go outside. Secure a garbage bag to the exterior dryer vent with masking tape.

6. Go inside. Reverse the vacuum's hose so it blows air instead of sucking it in.

7. Turn the vacuum on and blow air through the venting tube to force any trapped lint out of the vent and into the garbage bag.

8. Remove the garbage bag and resecure tube to dryer.

Highly flammable dryer lint is an excellent accelerant for lighting barbecues or campfires.

STEP 4

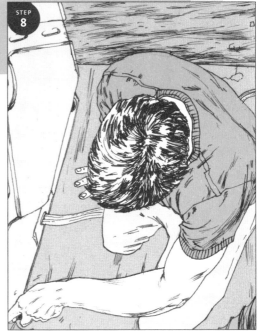

STEP 8

- All conventional dryers, whether gas or electric, use an electric fan to distribute the hot air that dries your clothes. Thus, even a "gas-powered" dryer consumes some electricity.

- To save energy, dry multiple loads one after the other to take advantage of the dryer drum's retained heat.

- Dryers located in a heated room (as opposed to a freezing garage) operate more efficiently.

- Using your washer's extended spin option will shorten the duration of the drying cycle and save energy, since dryers are more expensive to operate than washers.

- Dryers with a moisture sensor shut off automatically when clothes are dry, saving energy over models without one.

- Don't mix heavy and light items in the dryer. Dry towels separately.

- As the label says, clean the lint screen after each use.

- Check your vent once per year and clean it—or have it cleaned—as necessary.

- Install a flap-type closure on the exterior wall of your home where the exhaust tube vents to the outside. This keeps cold air out and prevents birds and other animals from getting in. The exhaust air forces the flaps open when the dryer is running.

- You've heard of the five hundred uses for dryer sheets? Have you also heard of the dozens of toxic chemicals they contain? Ditch the dryer sheets and try an antistatic ball.

GREEN UP YOUR DRY CLEANING

As a steward—or stewardess—of the environment, your goal should be to eliminate dry cleaning from your life. Period. Hand- or machine-wash everything you possibly can, and don't always believe the care instructions (see Green Bits, right). Admittedly, this is the ideal. The reality is more complicated. Some structured garments (suit jackets, especially) and synthetic fabrics just don't have an effective alternative to dry cleaning. So in the interests of eco-practicality, the following tips will help you reduce the negative environmental impact of this necessary evil.

AVOID PERC AT ALL COSTS

That "freshly dry-cleaned smell" you notice when you pick up your clothing is likely perchloro-ethylene, the most common solvent used in the traditional dry cleaning process. "Perc" can affect brain, liver, and kidney function, and it can cause headaches even after short-term exposure. In fact, perc is so toxic that in 2006, the EPA published new regulations requiring any dry cleaner located in a residential building to phase out its use by 2020. Ask your dry cleaner if the business uses it. If they do, find another one.

HANDLE DRY CLEANING LIKE TOXIC WASTE

OK, that's overstating it. But if you can't eliminate perc from your clothing, you can at least keep it out of your green home. First, remove the plastic wrapping from the clothes while you're still outside. Next, allow clothes to air out somewhere other than the home (in a garage, for example) for at least a day—preferably four or five days—before wearing them. Don't leave clothes in a small, enclosed space—such as hanging by the backseat of your car.

BE SKEPTICAL OF "ORGANIC" DRY CLEANING CLAIMS

Unlike, say, fruits and vegetables, there's no generally accepted definition of what constitutes "organic" when it comes to dry cleaning. You may notice a sign claiming that your dry cleaner has been "certified organic" by the Drycleaning & Laundry Institute (formerly the International Fabricare Institute). This is misleading. It simply indicates that the cleaner operates in an environmentally sound fashion—not necessarily that they don't use perc. One alternative solvent endorsed by the EPA is—believe it or not—carbon dioxide. Yes, it sounds environmentally dire, but in this case the CO_2 is pressurized to form a liquid. And it reportedly works better than perc anyway.

TRY HOME DRY CLEANING

Most of the so-called home dry cleaning products are of suspect efficacy: They make your clothing smell good, but their cleaning power is limited. Worse, they typically require using the dryer, which shouldn't really be your goal (though, environmentally speaking, it's probably better than dry cleaning). Still, you may find a brand that works for you. In general, these products should be used only for spot cleaning. They're fairly effective at removing water-based stains such as dirt and mud, but they tend not to work as well on oil-based or other stubborn stains. Mustard? Forget it.

- In 2007, California approved a plan to phase out all the state's dry cleaners' use of perc, which is on its list of toxic air contaminants. But that won't be until January 2023.

- Most men's dress shirts can be cold-water laundered and pressed or ironed.

- Wearing undershirts can reduce the need to dry-clean or launder shirts.

- The chemicals and high temperatures used in dry cleaning reduce the life of fabrics.

- Many sweaters with labels indicating "dry-clean only" can safely be hand-washed and laid flat to dry. This is especially true of cashmere, which doesn't react well to the stresses of dry cleaning.

- "Wrinkle-free" shirts are chemically treated.

CHEMICAL-FREE STAIN REMOVAL TIPS

12 QUICK FIXES

Most of the stains your kids are likely to create can be removed without the use of abrasive chemicals—unless they're playing with Sharpie markers or axle grease. One general rule of natural stain removal is "Be patient." Some of these tricks take time to work, while others may require two or even three applications for good results. Note that some stains (particularly permanent inks and dyes) often can't effectively be removed without chemicals. Or at all.

JUICE

Coat the stained area liberally with salt. Allow it to dry. Brush or vacuum off the salt. If the stain persists, mix one tablespoon of white vinegar with one-half cup of water, pour the solution onto the stain, then blot with a clean cloth.

CHEWING GUM

Freeze the gum using an ice cube, then remove as much of it as possible by hand. For any gum that remains, follow the steps for crayon.

BALLPOINT PEN INK

Blot washable fabrics with isopropyl (rubbing) alcohol, then blot them again with a clean cloth. Wash in cold water. Check the stain. If it remains, repeat. Don't use heat to dry the fabrics until the ink has disappeared. For non-washables, make a paste of (natural) laundry detergent and water, spread it on the stain, and allow to dry. Then vacuum. (Note: This removal method won't always work, and ink stains that have already set may be impossible to remove.)

CHOCOLATE

Soak the garment in cold water, then make and apply a paste as for grass. A persistent stain may require two applications.

DIRT

Rub natural liquid dish soap into the stain. Allow the garment to sit overnight, then wash normally. This also works for grass.

URINE

Make a solution of equal parts vinegar and water, blot the stain, then soak the garment in warm water or machine-wash it. If this isn't effective, dilute one-half cup of hydrogen peroxide with one cup of water and blot, then rinse the garment in cold water. Since urine is typically acidic and destroys fabric fibers, old stains are virtually impossible to remove.

CRAYON

Remove as much of the loose wax as possible by hand. Place a sheet of paper on the stain, then iron the paper with a warm iron. Shift the paper to a clean section and repeat, until all the crayon has melted and transferred to the paper. (Crayon on walls can be removed with a sponge soaked in vinegar—white, not balsamic.)

BLOOD

Put washable garments into the washing machine immediately. Wash on cold, using natural laundry detergent (see Unknown Stains, right, for detergent details). Do not tumble dry. Repeat until the stain disappears. For upholstery and rugs: Wet a clean cloth with cold water. Blot stain, shifting to a clean section of cloth until no more blood is transferred. Do not rub, and do not use warm or hot water. If the stain remains, mix one teaspoon natural laundry detergent with one cup water, soak cloth, then blot. If the stain persists, blot carefully with undiluted white vinegar. Avoid using excess water or other liquids, as you may be left with a water stain after removing the blood.

PENCIL MARKS

Use a gum eraser on non-machine washable garments; knead it well first. Blotting carefully with undiluted vinegar may also work.

GRASS

Mix one tablespoon of cornstarch with two teaspoons of water to make a paste. Rub the paste into the stain. Allow to dry, then vacuum or brush it off.

INDELIBLE INK

Typically, permanent markers and other indelible inks are impossible to remove from clothing and upholstery. However, on walls, scrubbing with undiluted white vinegar may lighten or remove the stain, depending on how fresh it is and how large an area it covers. If this method doesn't work, consider applying a fresh coat of paint. Then hide the Sharpies from the kids.

UNKNOWN STAINS

Stains can occasionally be removed by spot-treating with sodium percarbonate (sometimes called "oxygen bleach"). Though it's officially a chemical compound—of sodium carbonate and hydrogen peroxide—it is biodegradable and water-soluble. Sodium percarbonate is often the active ingredient in natural laundry detergents and those with "bleach alternatives." Still, the usual stain-treating caveat applies: Test a small, hidden area first before pouring on the compounds.

CHAPTER 7

THE BASEMENT
Utilities, Mechanicals, and Cold Storage

Of all the spaces in your soon-to-be-green home, the basement (or utility room, if you don't have a basement) is perhaps the easiest area to give an eco-makeover. A number of quick, affordable projects can save you money on utilities (insulating the water heater, turning the water temperature down) and reduce your waste stream (making flushable kitty litter). For the more ambitious—and those with a yen to dig up the floor—building your own root cellar and installing a geothermal heating and cooling system will keep you busy for a weekend. And when you get hungry and thirsty after all that work, you can eat some of your homegrown mushrooms—washed down with a glass of cabernet from your eco–wine cellar.

WRAP YOUR WATER HEATER WITH A SPACE BLANKET

Home water heaters are notorious energy hogs and energy wasters. Although modern heaters are insulated internally, even the most efficient units—those that are fully insulated, and those that recirculate hot water from the furnace instead of relying on a separate gas line—can be made more energy efficient with a tiny investment.

MATERIALS	$20

- ☐ Space (thermal) blanket, available at hardware and outdoor/camping stores
- ☐ Scissors
- ☐ Heat-reflective foil tape
- ☐ Tape measure
- ☐ Marker

You can buy a precut insulating blanket or "jacket" for about double the cost of a space blanket. (And you can have a plumber install it for another $100.) If you do buy one, make sure it has an insulating value of at least R-8. Before you install a new water heater, consider installing a "bottom board" under it. This piece of insulation will reduce heat loss from the tank into the floor.

STEPS TO WRAP THE HEATER

1. Measure the height and circumference of the water heater. Make sure the blanket will fit around it snugly. If the blanket is too big, cut it to fit. If it's too small, buy two and tape them end-to-end.

2. On the water heater, measure the size and position of any labels (especially those with model and serial numbers), thermostats, stickers, and emergency release and shutoff valves. By law, these shouldn't be obscured.

3. Draw cutouts of these items onto the space blanket, then remove the appropriate sections using the scissors.

4. Wrap the blanket around the heater. The reflective (shiny) side should face in. Secure it tightly with foil tape. (Don't substitute duct or other tape; it will crack.) Take extra care in insulating a gas-fed water heater: Make certain the burner isn't obstructed, and don't insulate the top, since it may interfere with the draft diverter.

5. Set the water heater temperature to less than 130°F to prevent overheating.

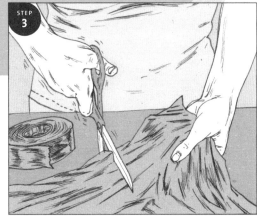

- Don't be fooled: Even a water heater that feels cool to the touch is dissipating heat over time, and thus wasting energy. The savings associated with using a blanket will vary based on your utility rates, water usage, and the ambient air temperature. But even a minimal savings of 10 cents per day (or $3 a month) will pay for the cost of the blanket in less than a year.

- You can save money by reducing the temperature of your hot water to 120°F. (If you have young children, you should do this anyway: Some units come from the factory with a default setting of 140°F, which is scalding.) Note, however, that at this low setting you may see a reduction in the cleaning efficiency of an older dishwasher without a heating booster. Scrape your dishes well.

PROPERLY STORE WINE AND BEER

Unless you live in northern Alaska or the Batcave, your basement is probably a little too warm—at least during the summer—for ideal wine and beer storage, which is 50–55°F. Nevertheless, you can take several steps to make it more usable, and to reduce the amount of cooling (energy) necessary for beer and white wine to reach their proper serving temperatures.

MATERIALS	$30

- ☐ Temperature and humidity gauge
- ☐ Clear tape
- ☐ Bricks or wood blocks
- ☐ Space (thermal) blanket (optional)
- ☐ Dehumidifier (optional)

If your basement is too warm to leave wine out, invest $200 in a small wine refrigerator, which is more efficient for its purpose than a large kitchen one and won't overchill.

- Beer should never be chilled, then allowed to warm, then rechilled.

- To chill a bottle of white wine quickly, put a half-dozen ice cubes into an insulated wine holder, add one cup of cold water, and place the bottle in the holder for fifteen minutes.

- Do not put a bottle of wine in the freezer: If you forget about it, it will crack.

STEPS TO STORE DRINKS

1. Check temperature and humidity. Red wine should never be stored in temperatures higher than 75°F, or it will turn. (If your basement is warmer than 60°F, see the Eco-cheat, left.) Humidity isn't as much of a problem, though high humidity (more than 65 percent) may encourage mold growth on the cork. Note, however, that excessively dry air may crack corks.

2. Locate a proper storage area. If the room doesn't have a dedicated thermostat, store the wine as close to the floor as possible, where cool air settles. Neither wine nor beer should be exposed to sunlight (use dark shades if a closet isn't available).

3. Position bottles. Wine, both red and white, should be stored on its side to keep the cork moist. This prevents cracking, which can allow air to enter the bottle and spoil the wine. Make sure the bottles are completely level. For red wine, this position also keeps the sediment on one side and away from the mouth of the bottle, where it might spoil the wine as it's poured. (In earthquake-prone regions, wine is sometimes stored with the neck tilted up slightly, to prevent the bottles from falling during seismic activity.) Cover wine labels with clear tape to protect them from moisture. Beer may be stored vertically. Unlike thicker wine bottles, beer bottles stacked horizontally in a "pyramid" may crack.

4. Use a space (thermal) blanket. Beer and wine bottles—and even a box containing the bottles—may be wrapped in a space blanket, shiny side facing out, to reflect ambient light and heat (see "Wrap Your Water Heater with a Space Blanket," page 112, for more information).

5. Bring wine and beer to the proper temperature before serving. Optimal temperatures for beer and wines vary, depending on the variety. As a general rule of thumb, beers should be served either very cold to cold (32–45°F) or at so-called cellar temperature (54–57°F), primarily for browns, bitters, and porters. White wines should be served very cold (champagne, sparkling wines) to cellar temperature (Sauternes). Red wines should be served at cellar temperature (Beaujolais, rosé) to medium cold (57–61°F, for Chianti, pinot noir) to room temperature (no higher than 65°F, for Bordeaux, Shiraz, cabernet, and other-full bodies varietals). When bringing your beverages up from the basement, chill beer and white wine in the refrigerator for an hour, and let red wine stand (decanted, if you choose) for an hour before serving.

Filling your home refrigerator with dozens of bottles of red and white wine wastes electricity: At about 40°F, most food refrigerators are much too cold for proper long-term wine storage.

115

CONSTRUCT A ROOT CELLAR

Before electricity was widely available, many people used root cellars to store perishable items such as fruits, vegetables, berries, and cured (though typically not raw) fish and meats. Root cellars take advantage of the earth's natural subterranean cooling properties and thus are emissions-free; they'll even save you the cost of refrigerating your produce.

MATERIALS	$250–$500, depending on size and depth

- ☐ Shovel or backhoe
- ☐ Four sheets of plywood, plus two-by-fours (for foundation)
- ☐ Concrete
- ☐ Cinder blocks and mortar
- ☐ 9-foot length of PVC pipe
- ☐ Metal shelving or, optionally, pressure-treated wood shelves
- ☐ Hammer and nails
- ☐ Thermometer and humidity gauge
- ☐ Gravel (optional)
- ☐ 1 sheet corrugated metal or plywood, for door

Big-box home-improvement stores sell prefabricated sheds that can be buried and used as root cellars. If you go this route, be sure to remove the shed's bottom, as a cool, damp floor is essential for a proper root cellar.

STEPS TO CONSTRUCT THE CELLAR

1. Determine placement: The easiest place to add a root cellar is under an existing, dirt-floor basement. However, a north- or east-facing slope that can be excavated is also an excellent choice. Avoid rocky or sandy terrain.

2. Determine depth: At a depth of about 12 feet in damp soil, the earth's temperature is cool and relatively stable. Of course, you probably won't be building a root cellar if you live in a desert, since high humidity is essential for long-term food storage. Check the locations of buried pipes and cables before digging (utility companies should tell you for free).

3. Excavate: There's no ideal size for a root cellar. However, plan on at least 6 x 8 x 12 feet deep for a reasonable amount of storage space.

4. Assemble the foundation: Using the plywood and two-by-fours, build wood forms to support the poured concrete as it sets. The foundation should be 16 inches thick and at least 1 foot high. (If building into a hillside, you can use logs in place of concrete and cinder blocks. Place them on rocks to prevent rot.)

5. Mix and pour concrete into the foundation forms. Allow it to dry completely, at least a few days.

6. Build walls: Stack and mortar cinder blocks for walls. If it's in your basement, you'll enter your root cellar from the top, using a ladder. If in a hillside, leave the north- or east-facing side open, for a door. The bottom of the room is likely to be damp, which is necessary for an effective root cellar. If it's wet, cover it with 3 to 6 inches of gravel. (You can buy premade cellars—typically constructed of corrugated metal—that can be assembled in the excavated space; see the Eco-cheat, previous page)

7. Add a vent: If the root cellar is built into a hillside, dig a hole in the ceiling and insert the PVC pipe into it to act as a vent for warm air and off-gassing from the food. If it's in a basement, cut a vent hole into the roof (see Step 9).

8. Place shelving against walls. You may be able to find old wire shelving at garage or sidewalk sales or junk shops.

9. Add a door (or roof, if it's below your basement). The door or roof should be made of thick planks, preferably pressure-treated, or corrugated metal.

10. Monitor temperature and humidity levels for a week. Ideally, you'll want your root cellar to be no warmer than 55°F. Some fruits and vegetables (apples, carrots, cucumbers, eggplant, cantaloupe) prefer colder storage conditions, typically less than 40°F. Ideal humidity conditions vary depending on the produce stored. As a general rule, most fruits and vegetables (including apples, pears, grapes, potatoes, carrots, beets, broccoli, radishes, and brussels sprouts) do better in moderately high to high humidity (70–90 percent). Garlic, onions, and peppers prefer drier air.

11. Add appropriate items to your root cellar.

12. Monitor temperature. If the outside air drops below the temperature of the cellar, open the door at night (except if it drops below freezing). Pack root vegetables (especially potatoes) in sawdust to preserve them. Keep the door closed as much as possible.

STEP
6

STEP
9

STEP
11

119

ASSEMBLE A GEOTHERMAL SYSTEM

Until someone figures out how to warm a building using wishful thinking, geothermal heat exchange is likely to remain the most energy-efficient method to heat (and cool) a home. This is because geothermal systems don't use fossil fuels (oil, coal, natural gas) or nuclear power to generate the energy needed to create heat—and they don't require the transmission of electricity to your home. Instead, they're self-contained and take advantage of a very handy, naturally occurring phenomenon. Below the frost line, the earth's interior temperature remains relatively constant throughout the year, warmer than the air above it in winter and cooler in summer—like a cave. Although their initial installation cost can be high, geothermal heating-cooling systems typically pay for themselves—in the form of greatly reduced energy bills—in as little as five years.

MATERIALS	$10,000 or greater, depending on home size and local geology

- ☐ Jackhammer, pickax, and shovels, plus several stout helpers
- ☐ Commercial borer
- ☐ Geothermal earth connection
- ☐ Geothermal heat pump subsystem
- ☐ Geothermal heat distribution system

STEPS TO ASSEMBLE THE SYSTEM

1. Locate the frost line. The earth's frost line varies based on geographic location, as well as factors such as hydrology and geology. Typically, local building codes will specify the exact depth of the frost line, because most foundations must be set below this level to avoid damage from frost heave.

2. Begin digging. For basement installation, use the jackhammer to break up concrete flooring, then pickaxes and shovels to break up

In general, it's much cheaper to purchase a new home with a geothermal system already installed—where the cost is built into your mortgage—than to retrofit an existing structure. In addition, suburban homes with larger plots are more likely to support trench or coil piping systems, which are easier and less expensive to install. In most cases, installing a geothermal transfer system isn't a do-it-yourself affair: You'll need a professional installer (or several of them), as well as a civil and structural engineer. However, you can save money by researching your area's water table level, soil composition, and zoning laws regarding deep-hole drilling, if applicable.

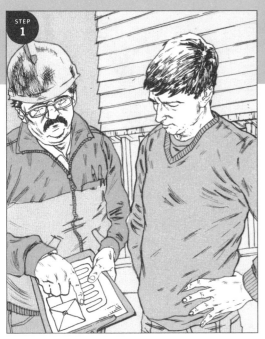

and remove rocks and soil. For smaller homes with low acreage, a vertical (rather than a horizontal, or "trench") loop system should be used. Using a borer, drill to a depth of 150–250 feet.

3. Insert the piping (the connection system). The piping will carry fluid—typically, water, or a combination of water and antifreeze—into the ground to absorb heat and return it to the surface and into your home.

4. Connect the piping to the heat pump. The geothermal heat pump removes the heat from the piping and concentrates it as hot air for more efficient use, via a compressor, a condenser, and an expansion valve system. (It's the same process used by your refrigerator, except in reverse.) The underground piping serves as the evaporator in the winter, to absorb heat from the earth and begin the process again.

5. Connect the heat pump to the distribution system. Typically, traditional ductwork and a fan or air handler are used to force hot air through the home instead of hot water, which is a less efficient means of heat distribution. Some systems can also transfer the heat pump's water directly to the home's hot water tank using a desuperheater.

Geothermal heating systems are pricier than traditional oil and gas furnaces—even highly efficient ones. (A typical three-ton residential geothermal system costs about $7,500, versus about $4,000 for a furnace or central air conditioner.) However, savings on utilities can be as high as 70 percent, and in some cases utility companies may actually pay you for using a geothermal system, because it reduces demand on their grid during peak heating and cooling periods. Contact your local utility company to inquire about rebates, which may be significant.

GROW MUSHROOMS IN A DAMP BASEMENT

Yes, mushrooms are easier to grow than weeds. And they taste better. No, they don't require manure—though you may find they grow faster and in more copious amounts in this nutrient-rich substrate. They do require a dark, moist room in which to spawn, so a damp basement should do nicely. Once the mycelium (the name for the body of the fungus, sometimes called "spawn" by professionals) begins to grow, it will continue to do so indefinitely, with minimal care, as long as the mycelium itself isn't damaged. Keep in mind that vermin may be attracted to mushrooms, so consider hoisting your growing medium off the floor.

MATERIALS	$50

- ☐ Growing substrate: 7–10 pounds of sawdust, shredded straw, finely ground wood chips, or coffee grounds
- ☐ Vat of boiling water
- ☐ Plastic wrap
- ☐ Knife
- ☐ Mushroom spawn (available online for less than $25)
- ☐ Charcoal-filtered gas mask (recommended)
- ☐ Damp basement

You can purchase spores and preinoculated logs online at www.fungi.com and www.sporestore.com. For logs, soak them overnight and then place them in your basement.

STEPS TO GROW THE MUSHROOMS

1. Boil the substrate for 5 minutes to saturate and sterilize it completely. (Damp, used coffee grounds from your coffeemaker are *not* sterile, though they probably don't contain harmful chemicals.)

2. Remove substrate and allow it to cool until it can be handled.

3. Put on the gas mask. (If you're not using a mask, the following should be performed outside.) Mix the purchased spawn with the substrate material (called "inoculation"). Depending on the type of mushroom and where spawn was purchased, it may already be mixed with substrate material. If so, just mix this in with your added material.

4. Form the inoculated substrate into a mound on a long sheet of plastic wrap, then cover it tightly with more wrap to form a log. Wrap it a second time to seal. Form several logs until all the substrate has been used.

5. Prick each log with a sharp knife several dozen times. The holes should be no less than 1/4 inch apart. Place the logs in your damp basement. To reduce the possibility that rodents or insects will eat your mushrooms before you do, consider tying the inoculated log with rope and suspending it from a ceiling beam.

6. Turn the light off.

7. Wait five days.

8. Pick mushrooms, rinse them, and prepare as you would store-bought fungi. Freshly picked mushrooms will rot immediately if not refrigerated (in a paper bag) or dried.

- If you have access to a damp wooded area *and* a mushroom expert, you can collect inoculated logs and bring them home to your damp basement. However, be warned that many poisonous and nonpoisonous mushrooms look alike, so this method isn't recommended unless you identify and collect mushrooms with a mycelium expert.

- Some mushroom varieties will grow only in highly specific humidity ranges and elevations.

- Good choices for basement mushrooms include pearl oysters, shiitakes, cinnamon caps, shaggymanes, morels, and chanterelles.

MAKE ENVIRONMENTALLY SOUND KITTY LITTER

Few cats can be trained to use the toilet. Flushing? Forget it. And even if your tom-cat could, he'd probably leave the seat up. Flushable cat litter—which is treated the same as human waste—is more environmentally friendly than traditional litter, which gets dumped in a landfill. However, it's also more expensive, as well as messy to transport to the toilet. The following homemade recipe is inexpensive, will keep kitty happy and regular, and is environmentally benign.

MATERIALS	$10

- ☐ 1 pound of baking soda
- ☐ 5–7 pounds of sawdust or fine wood chips
- ☐ Trash can
- ☐ Plastic litter box

STEPS TO MAKE THE LITTER

1. Combine baking soda with 1 cup of cold water. Mix thoroughly until you have a paste.

2. In a large trash can, combine baking soda paste with 5–7 pounds of sawdust or wood chips. Mix well. Both products are available from landscapers, or at garden stores and lumberyards, at minimal cost. A friendly arborist may also give you as much as you can carry, for free.

3. Spread litter mixture on newspapers and allow to air-dry for one to two days.

For faster results—or if you find kitty is leaving tiny white paw prints on the carpet—eliminate the baking soda and just use freshly chipped wood or sawdust. Replace it after one week—or when you can no longer stand the smell.

- Used biodegradable cat litter is an excellent means to get rid of garden moles. Just dump it into their holes and cover them with soil.

- On average, Americans dump eight billion pounds of kitty litter into landfills each year—twice the amount, by weight, of disposable diapers.

4. Scoop up the litter and use it normally. The baking soda will absorb most—though not all—of the odor and reduce the acidity of the urine. Remove solid waste every few days and flush (composting isn't recommended). Once the litter is fully saturated—about two weeks—it's fully biodegradable.

CHAPTER 8

THE GARAGE
Smart Transportation

Stop driving. Not just right now. Forever.

There, I said it. Now I feel better. OK, so this isn't going to happen. And the garage projects in this chapter acknowledge (reluctantly) that it's not going to happen. We need to drive, some of us more than others, and the gas-powered car isn't going to disappear anytime soon. (The oil needed to power it might, but that's another story.) But there are ways to drive better, smarter, and faster—wait, not that last one. In this section, you'll learn how to get maximum fuel efficiency from your non hybrid vehicle, how to make your hybrid even more efficient than it already is, how to use your car to save electricity, how other modes of transportation stack up against the automobile, and how to make your garage itself more energy efficient. And who knows? Maybe after reading you'll be inspired to sell the Excursion and buy a Tahoe. They're practically giving them away now.

GET THE MOST MILEAGE FROM YOUR NON-HYBRID

If you don't already own a hybrid, well … why not? OK, realistically lots of people require larger vehicles—for work, for their four kids—or simply aren't ready or able to replace their car, truck, or fuel-gulping Escalade. So what's a green-conscious driver to do? Drive less, for one thing, and take public transportation more. If you must drive, however, follow these dos and don'ts to improve your vehicle's fuel economy.

DO DRIVE SLOWER

The single easiest way to improve fuel economy is to drive slower. At highway speeds, every ten miles per hour over 60 mph reduces fuel economy by about four miles per gallon (mpg)— a figure that remains fairly constant regardless of vehicle size. Need more motivation? Look at it another way: If gas costs $3.25 per gallon, every 10 mph you drive over 60 mph is the equivalent of gas going up 54 cents per gallon. Gulp.

DON'T SPEED

Speeding saves very little time and costs a lot of money. One recent study found that a car driven aggressively for ninety miles saved barely five minutes over a smoothly driven car—and used 30 percent more fuel. (Of course, on a nine-hundred-mile trip, you'll save more time, provided you don't get pulled over for speeding. Or crash.) Visit www.drive55.org for information on how much speeding costs you.

DON'T WORRY ABOUT USING THE AIR CONDITIONER

The old saw about turning off the AC to save fuel is essentially a myth. At 65 mph—and depending on road conditions—you may save 1 mpg, but that's it.

DON'T WORRY ABOUT OPEN WINDOWS

Another maxim says that driving with the windows open disrupts a car's aerodynamics, hurting fuel economy. Unless you're driving a stretch limo with twenty yards of windows rolled down, the difference in mileage is negligible.

DON'T WORRY UNNECESSARILY ABOUT THE AIR FILTER

Years ago, when air and fuel ratios weren't regulated by microchips, there was some truth to the claim that a dirty air filter hurt fuel economy. Today, this is no longer the case. Still, you shouldn't drive forever on a single filter: Change it every ten thousand miles or so.

DO TRY TO COAST

Because of inertia, car engines have to work much harder—and use more fuel—to move a car from a standstill than to keep a moving vehicle moving. (That's why gasoline-powered car engines are less efficient in the city than on the highway.) Whenever it's possible and safe, try to anticipate red lights and keep the car moving until the light turns green.

DON'T BOTHER WAITING UNTIL MIDNIGHT TO FILL UP THE TANK

Because cooler gasoline is denser than hot gasoline, many people believe they'll get more gas for their money if they avoid filling up the tank when it's hot outside. In fact, studies show that the temperature of the gas as it leaves the pump nozzle changes very little, if at all, in the course of a day.

DON'T MAKE JACKRABBIT STARTS

Stomping on the accelerator pedal when the light turns green burns lots of gas—not to mention the rubber on your tires.

DO KEEP YOUR TIRES PROPERLY INFLATED

Driving on underinflated tires not only hurts fuel mileage but also affects maneuverability, which can lead to accidents. Check your tire pressure monthly, and don't forget that the pressure varies with the ambient air temperature and the load. Check your car's manual—not the tire sidewall—for proper inflation recommendations.

DO USE CRUISE CONTROL

On flat roads, cruise control keeps the car at a consistent speed and eliminates jerky throttle application, both of which help overall fuel economy.

DO USE THE PROPER-OCTANE GASOLINE

Technically, any modern car's ignition system is sophisticated enough to retard spark plug timing based on the octane level of fuel. (Preignition causes the dreaded "knocking" in the engine.) However, any savings you gain when you pay for slightly cheaper gas may be lost in reduced fuel economy. And you'll definitely notice a decrease in performance. Besides, if you're driving a $50,000 car and can't afford gas that's 10 cents more per gallon, it's time to sell the Benz and buy a Prius.

DO ORDER FEWER OPTIONS WITH YOUR NEW CAR

One of the easiest and cheapest ways to increase fuel economy is to reduce weight. Those expensive gewgaws you thought you couldn't live without—the twenty-inch dubs, the fifty-way adjustable heated and cooled and shiatsu massaging seats, the greenhouse-size sunroof—all these options add extra weight, which translates to decreased fuel economy.

BOND WITH YOUR HYBRID

You dumped the Cherokee and bought the Civic hybrid. Sure, you spent two years on a waiting list—and while you waited the tax credit expired. Now, though, you're at the mercy of all those high-ridin' SUVs you once counted among your automotive peers. And you've got their headlights *right* in your eyes. It's time for a little green vehicle love-in with your new best friend. Take the following steps to become one with your twenty-first-century econobox.

GET A VANITY PLATE

Choose something that sends a message to other drivers while at the same time conveying your self-satisfaction: "45MPG" or "GASSIPPR" or "DRIVE55" are good choices.

GET A BUMPER STICKER WITH A MESSAGE

Consider "My Other Car Is My Feet" or "Drive It Like Gas Costs $10/Gallon—Because It Will Soon" or "45MPG Patriot."

REVIEW YOUR FUEL RECEIPTS IN BED

If you use a gas card, you'll get an itemized accounting of how much fuel you're buying—and if you track your mileage, you'll know how far you're going on a tank. Go over the numbers to help you relax before falling asleep. If you're having trouble, count miles per gallon instead of sheep.

SLEEP WITH THE KEY FOB UNDER YOUR PILLOW

If you wake up during the night, reach under the pillow and lovingly caress the keys. Or walk outside and chirp the alarm once or twice to make certain everything's OK.

DRIVE IN THE CITY

Stopping at red lights saves fuel, because the car's gasoline engine shuts down. And with regenerative braking, stepping on the brake pedal recharges the batteries, which also saves gas. These are two reasons why hybrids tend to get better mileage in the city than on the highway.

ENTER A "HYPERMILING" CONTEST

These competitions pit hybrid owners against one another in a quest to achieve the most miles per gallon; some drivers have claimed to hit the near-mythical 100 mpg. See www.hypermiling.com for details.

COAST

Drive your hybrid down a hill and grin with satisfaction as the car's motor shuts down.

GET SOCIAL REINFORCEMENT

Visit www.greenhybrid.com to track your mileage online with thousands of other hybrid fanatics. (The Toyota Prius is the current miles-per-gallon leader with forty-eight, followed by the Honda Civic Hybrid with forty-six.)

CONVERT YOUR HYBRID TO RUN ON (MORE) ELECTRICITY

Hybrid cars have relatively low emissions and get great gas mileage—when compared to, say, a Hummer. But judge one against a fully electric car and the savings are, well . . . there aren't any. Although most automakers killed their electric cars some years ago (see "Alternative Vehicles: Hybrids, Scooters, and Electric Cars," page 134), with higher gas prices likely in the future electric vehicles may yet rise from the ashes. But if you already own a hybrid and don't want to wait, there's one promising option: conversion.

HOW IT WORKS

The Hymotion L5 Plug-in Conversion Module is being developed by a123 Systems, a company that designs advanced lithium-ion batteries for cars. The kit converts a hybrid electric vehicle (HEV) like the Prius to a plug-in hybrid electric vehicle (PHEV). In essence, the kit is a very large, computer-controlled battery pack that is added to the Prius's existing battery and is charged by standard 120-volt household current. It's designed to allow the car to travel for longer distances using more electric (battery) power and less gasoline. The company claims that a PHEV Prius can achieve more than 100 mpg over a range of thirty to forty miles—more than twice the mileage of a standard HEV.

HOW MUCH WILL YOU SAVE?

The conversion kit costs about $10,000. Unless oil prices are well above $100 a barrel, the kit isn't likely to pay for itself in fuel savings alone over the life of the car. However, if it works as advertised, it could reduce emissions significantly. According to the company's calculations:

A commuter who drives twelve thousand miles per year (70 percent city and 30 percent highway miles), has a daily thirty-mile commute, and recharges his or her car at work will reap the following benefits:

- Achieve 111 combined mpg (compared with 47 mpg for a standard Prius)
- Consume 108 gallons of fuel per year (compared with 255 for a standard Prius)
- Make only nine yearly trips to the gas station (standard Prius: twenty one)
- Emit 2,097 pounds of CO_2 annually (standard Prius: 4,943 pounds)
- Emit 110 pounds of other greenhouse gases (260 for a standard Prius)

THE DRAWBACKS

Cost, obviously, is the primary impediment to adoption of this technology. Of course, when gas prices rise, the conversion kits become more attractive financially. But electricity, too, isn't free, and fossil fuels add to air pollution and greenhouse gas emissions—and unlike a fully electric car, a PHEV still uses gasoline. Further, electricity prices are likely to continue to rise, offsetting some of the gains promised by the Hymotion. The kit's battery also requires five hours to charge completely, which limits ownership to those with ready access to a power outlet while at work.

THE VERDICT

If you (a) already own a Prius; (b) would rather drive alone than carpool or take public transportation; (c) have a fairly short commute from the suburbs, where you also have a garage; and (d) have a spare $10,000, then you should visit www.a123systems.com/hymotion/home and send in your deposit. Otherwise, reduce your emissions by driving less.

- As I write this, another company, EDrive Systems is planning to soon launch a similar, competing technology. Like the Hymotion, EDrive claims that its conversion kit will offer 100-plus mpg in a Prius, over short distances and at moderate speeds. But according to the company, a depleted EDrive battery will require six hours to recharge. The cost for a full charge, assuming approximately 10 cents per kilowatt-hour (on average), would be about $1. Visit www.edrivesystems.com for details.

- Automakers—especially Toyota and Honda—are working on their own versions of PHEVs; new models are expected to arrive within several years. Owing to economies of scale, these cars are likely to be cheaper, overall, than adding an aftermarket PHEV kit to a hybrid car. And the warranties will be longer.

ALTERNATIVE VEHICLES: HYBRIDS, SCOOTERS, AND ELECTRIC CARS

If you want zero-emissions transportation, try a bicycle. Or your feet. But these solutions are typically practical only for short distances. What if your commute is twenty miles? Hybrid gasoline-electric vehicles are obviously less polluting than traditional cars powered only by internal combustion engines. But how do they measure up to, say, a scooter? Or an electric car?

HOW THEY COMPARE

- A Prius averaging a very respectable 45 mpg would use 266 gallons of fuel to travel twelve thousand miles in a year. A scooter with a single rider averaging a typical 60 mpg would use two hundred gallons per year to go the same twelve thousand miles. (And some small scooters can achieve 100 mpg. Granted, a scooter can carry only two people, but many commuter cars don't carry more than two passengers, either.)

- One study has found that scooters, owing to their superior fuel economy, reduce emissions by approximately 0.4 pounds per mile versus the average car. When applied to driving twelve thousand miles per year, this equates to about 4,800 pounds of emissions.

- Electric cars—and there are still a few available in the used market, mostly in California—are classified as zero-emissions vehicles (ZEVs). ZEVs produce no emissions from the vehicle itself, but of course the electricity used to power them does. Using conventional power sources, a hybrid car produces about three hundred grams of greenhouse gas emissions per mile traveled. Using conventional power, a ZEV would produce slightly less than fifty grams of emissions over the same mile—a significant reduction. However, if 100 percent renewable power (wind, solar) is used in place of conventional fuel (coal and gas), emissions to power a ZEV fall to virtually zero.

Looking for high mileage? Hemp stalks are rich in fiber and cellulose and therefore could potentially be used in power generation. Hemp stalk can be converted to a charcoal-like substance through a process called pyrolysis. In fact, Henry Ford (yes, him again) was a pioneer in pyrolysis: He operated a biomass pyrolytic plant at Iron Mountain in northern Michigan and even produced a hemp-fueled car! (No record on whether the tailpipe emissions were, um, medicinal.)

REVIVING THE ELECTRIC CAR

- From the late 1990s to 2005, Honda, Toyota, Nissan, Chrysler, Ford, and General Motors all built electric cars because of a California mandate—about five thousand were ultimately manufactured. But cheap gasoline plus a lack of serious marketing ultimately killed the electric car: four thousand were reportedly crushed. Automakers claimed that buyers weren't interested in paying a premium for a car that had a range of just one hundred miles per charge. At least not when gas was cheap. And yet, the average American driver travels only thirty-four miles in a day; 85 percent of Americans travel less than fifty miles per day.

- The GM EV1, an electric car introduced in 1996, went from 0 to 60 mph in 7.4 seconds, had a top speed of 140 mph, and a range of 120 miles. It's no longer in production.

- Chevrolet has announced the concept Chevy Volt, which the company claims will run on gas, electricity, E85 ethanol, or biodiesel. Production is scheduled for 2010.

- Tesla Motors is now producing the fully electric Tesla Roadster, which can achieve the equivalent of 200 mpg, can travel two hundred miles on a single charge, and goes from zero to sixty in a neck-snapping 3.9 seconds. The price? More than $100,000. But think of all the gas money you'll save! Visit www.teslamotors.com to place your order.

Think driving is more convenient than public transit? It may be, but it's also much more expensive. Factor in time wasted in traffic, and you're saving very little of anything— and you're spewing *way* more emissions. Fortunately, those clever folks at Google have created a Web site that gives you step-by-step (or stop-by-stop) public transportation directions for select cities. For details visit www.google.com/transit.

CONVERT YOUR CAR TO RUN ON GREASE

With fairly minor modifications, any diesel-powered car can run on used vegetable oil, aka grease. These "grease cars" are distinct from cars powered by biodiesel, which is a chemically engineered fuel that must be purchased retail. The benefits of the grease car are numerous: Used vegetable oil is free (restaurants like to give it away because otherwise they pay disposal fees to have it removed), grease is less polluting than diesel fuel, conversion kits are cheap, mileage is equivalent, and the engine isn't altered. And grease cars can—and typically must—also run on plain old diesel.

MATERIALS	$1,750, on average

- ☐ Diesel-powered car (new or used, turbo or naturally aspirated)
- ☐ Vegetable fuel system conversion kit (available from www.greasecar.com and other places)
- ☐ Shade tree or professional mechanic
- ☐ New or gently used vegetable or soybean oil

You can save the costs—and, let's be honest, the mess—of installing a vegetable fuel system in your car by buying a used grease car. Many are available for less than $5,000—plus the cost of grease. For listings visit www.greasecar.com/clasi.cfm

STEPS TO CONVERT YOUR CAR

1. Examine the conversion kit and read instructions carefully. Typical kits include a fuel cell and grease tank, solenoid fuel valve, thermal filter, heated fuel lines, and the required fittings and couplings. Prices range from about $1,000 at the low end to $2,500 at the high end, depending on vehicle make and engine displacement.

2. Choose self- or professional installation. Vegetable fuel systems are relatively simple to install for a professional mechanic or an experienced wrench turner. If you bring your car to the dealer for an oil change, choose professional installation. Installation costs range from $1,200 to about $1,500.

3. Install the kit. Refer to the installation instructions, or pay for installation.

4. Understand how the system works. Typical vegetable fuel cars simply replace diesel fuel in the engine with heated grease, with no engine modifications necessary. That's the good news. The not-so-good news is that,

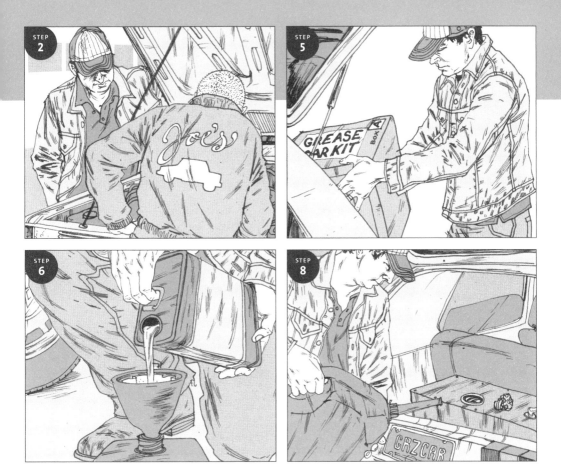

- What about hydrogen power? Several automakers are set to release (admittedly expensive) hydrogen-fueled vehicles, which produce zero tailpipe emissions. One problem is that very few hydrogen refueling stations exist, and the ones that do are mostly in—where else?—California. Another, perhaps larger issue is that the overall emissions benefits of generating hydrogen—a process that, at least currently, requires fossil fuels—are questionable.

- Grease car proponents claim that, when used as fuel, vegetable oil is carbon neutral: That is, the plants absorb more carbon dioxide as they grow than is released into the air when their oil is combusted in an engine. Diesel fuel isn't guilt-free, though. It burns hotter than gasoline, and it produces more nitrogen oxides, which contribute to smog—one reason California has very strict diesel emissions regulations.

because vegetable oil, unlike diesel, is solid at room temperature, it must be heated to about 140°F before it can be used to power the car. For this reason, grease cars run on standard diesel fuel after start-up for as little as five minutes and a few miles—or for much longer, if the air temperature is very cold. They also must be switched back to diesel before shut-down, to ensure that no vegetable oil is left in the fuel lines, where it might solidify. Conversion kits include a switch to make the change from one to the other. (You may also want to purchase a heat exchanger to heat the grease up more quickly.)

5. Acquire grease. Unless you're going to pay for new vegetable oil, used vegetable or soybean oil that has been changed frequently (once a week) is your best bet. In terms of suppliers, high-quality Asian restaurants are good choices because they use lots of oil for deep frying and presumably change it regularly.

6. Filter. To operate a grease car reliably, you must filter the oil to remove impurities (and water) that can cause engine malfunction. You can use inexpensive paper oil filters, or buy a garage or in-car filtration system.

7. Disinfect the grease. Vegetable oil must be stored in sealed containers, because it's prone to bacterial growth. Products such as Sea Foam (www.seafoamsales.com) help to clean the oil, reduce moisture, and inhibit bacterial growth during storage.

8. Fill the grease tank and drive normally. When properly cared for, a vegetable oil–fueled car shouldn't see any reduction in mileage or power. Naturally, driving such a car isn't as simple as turning a key—grease cars are probably best suited to those who are mechanically inclined and not afraid of, well, getting greasy.

Note: Pure vegetable oil hasn't been approved by the EPA as a motor fuel and hasn't passed the necessary Clean Air Act requirements for automobile fuel. Further, using it in your new car is almost certain to void much of the warranty—or at the very least, those parts that cover the fuel system and related components.

- One company has created a home refueling station that synthesizes ethanol, the gasoline replacement currently in vogue. Although the economic and emissions benefits of ethanol are debatable, if you've got a warehouse full of sugar—it takes twelve pounds to make one gallon of home brew ethanol—and $10,000, you might as well consider throwing it all at your SUV. Visit www.efuel100.com for details.

- In general, when combusted in a car, grease is cleaner-burning than diesel fuel. In fact, it contains no sulfur at all.

- If you like the idea of a cleaner car but aren't ready to root around Dumpsters in search of grease, consider biodiesel. Pure biodiesel isn't the same as food-grade vegetable oil and is an approved fuel for vehicles. It has much lower emissions than either diesel or gasoline, doesn't come from a finite resource like petroleum, and can be purchased from retailers instead of synthesized. However, because it's taxed like gas, it costs more than cheap (or in some cases free) grease.

SEGWAY VERSUS ELECTRIC BIKE: CHOOSING A COOL COMMUTER VEHICLE

If a hybrid car still strikes you as essentially an SUV without the guilt, then you're probably in the target demographic for the Segway and the electric bike. Both can get you to work on time without breaking a sweat (in theory, anyway), and both look cool. And both completely eliminate gasoline from the equation. While neither offers the speed, range, protection, and climate-controlled comfort of a car, for short distances both are very eco-friendly choices. But which one's right for your green garage?

SEGWAY

The Segway has developed a devoted, if fairly specialized, following. By now, you've probably seen Segway-based urban tour groups, the "Segway security guard," and even the occasional trailblazing "Segway senior." But what about a Segway as a zero-emissions commuter vehicle? The company claims significant environmental benefits in the form of reduced emissions and air pollution. And these claims are accurate, if one is comparing a Segway to a car (even a hybrid). But, in truth, if you can swap a Segway for your car to get to work or meander around town, you can probably swap the Segway for a bus, a bike, or your sneakers.

SEGWAY POSITIVES

- The Segway is a zero-emissions vehicle.
- You can legally drive a Segway indoors (with permission).
- For short trips for a single person, a Segway is more energy efficient than any car, save an electric vehicle.
- Even adjusting for emissions from the generation of power used to charge a Segway, it still offers a 71 percent reduction in CO_2 emissions versus a scooter, and a 93 percent reduction versus the average U.S. passenger car.
- You'll look cool, depending on whom you talk to.

SEGWAY NEGATIVES

- You can't legally drive a Segway on a highway (or even a parkway), negating its utility as a commuter device, except for city dwellers.
- Laws on where a Segway can be legally driven vary by state and even municipality.
- Segways are heavy (one hundred pounds or more) and have a limited range (about twenty-five miles on a charge).
- A Segway can travel as fast as (or faster than) a bike, but it isn't as maneuverable at high speeds.
- Segways don't perform well on side slopes.
- Segways are expensive when compared to their true competition: the electric bike.
- You may be taken for a geek, depending on whom you talk to.

ELECTRIC BIKE

Not long ago, a sturdy, reliable electric bike cost many thousands of dollars. (Some lightweight, high-end models still do.) But prices have dropped considerably, and today you can buy an electric bike for less than $500 at, of all places, Walmart. Unlike a Segway, an electric bike is really an electrically assisted vehicle, so it can be used with or without the motor. Its range is thus infinite, or at least limited only by your energy, not the battery's.

ELECTRIC BIKE POSITIVES

- Price. An electric bike such as the $350 E-Zip Trailz (www.currietech.com) costs less than a tenth of a new Segway.

- Charge time. The lead-acid batteries used in low-end electric bikes can be fully charged in three hours, versus up to ten for the Segway's lithium-ion battery.

- Range. As noted, an electrically assisted bike can be driven without the use of the motor. When using the battery-driven motor for, say, going up hills, the charge will still last for up to about twenty miles.

- Emissions. Like a Segway, an electric bike produces no tailpipe emissions; emissions are only those from electricity generation in the power grid.

ELECTRIC BIKE NEGATIVES

- Low-end (in other words, cheap) electric bikes typically use environmentally unsound lead-acid batteries, and many are guaranteed for only a year. Further, the manufacturers may not recycle them, though there are programs in the United States that will (see "Reduce Remote Control Battery Usage," page 48).

- Laws vary by state but, unlike standard bicycles, electric bikes may be considered "motorized vehicles," which means they often require a special driver's license, plus registration fees.

- Electric bikes are heavy—particularly cheap electric bikes, which can weigh more than fifty pounds. This makes transporting them (not to mention pedaling them) a chore.

THE VERDICT

From an emissions standpoint, any electric vehicle looks like a winner when compared to a car, hybrid or not. The Segway is marketed as a replacement for a car, but in reality it's neither a commuter vehicle nor a grocery hauler—and in some states it isn't legal to pilot one on the road, period. An electric bike, by contrast, can be used on streets, making it appropriate for hilly commutes. For those with trouble walking, a Segway would be more appropriate than any bike. But for everyone else, an electric bike offers equal or greater speed and range, better maneuverability, and more versatility for a lot less money. And it's still a conversation piece.

INSULATE YOUR GARAGE DOOR

Unless you're a car fanatic with a stable of expensive rides, you probably don't have a fully insulated garage. And even if your garage walls are insulated—a possibility in newer homes—the garage door almost certainly is not. An attached garage that's closer to the interior temperature of your home can lower your utility bills significantly. And for less than $200 you can insulate the door yourself.

MATERIALS	$200

- ☐ Garage door (metal, fiberglass, or wood)
- ☐ Garage door insulation kit (available at home-improvement stores) or rolled foil insulation
- ☐ Tape measure
- ☐ Straight edge
- ☐ Matte knife or tin snips

A well-insulated metal garage door can reflect more than 90 percent of the door's radiant heat, keeping the garage cool in summer and reducing the load on your central air conditioner

STEPS TO INSULATE THE DOOR

1. Measure door. Most garage doors are 7 feet high by 9 feet wide; doubles are 7 by 16 feet. The kits typically include panels to fit these dimensions. If your door is an odd size, you can either try to find a kit with the matching size or cut the kit's panels to fit.

2. Check insulation. Kits usually include an insulation layer between a layer of foil and a layer of foam.

3. Cut it if necessary. The insulation should come precut into standard panels to fit the height and width of the door. If it isn't, or if you're using rolled insulation, measure and cut the insulation pieces to fit, using the matte knife or tin snips. The insulation should be cut to fit between the hinged sections of the door.

4. Mount it. Use the kit's included adhesive strips to mount the panels on the garage door. The foil side should face the door. The easiest way to mount the panels is to start at the top of the door and then roll the door up as you go, so you don't have to kneel. This will also help you make sure the insulation doesn't interfere with the door's opening or closing.

5. Trim it. Cut away any excess insulation.

STEP 1

STEP 3

STEP 4

- A detached garage doesn't need insulation, unless you use it as a workroom or office— or live in a very cold climate where subzero winter temperatures make starting your car difficult.

- Painting the outside of the garage door a light color can help keep the inside cooler.

USE YOUR CAR TO CHARGE COMMON HOUSEHOLD ITEMS

Clearly, you're not going to power, say, your home's dishwasher or plasma TV by plugging them into your Prius. But that doesn't mean you can't be creative when it comes to saving electricity by charging things with your car. Use the following tips to get the most power from your ride while eliminating the wall outlet from the equation. (These tips work for both hybrids and conventional gasoline-powered vehicles.)

CHARGE WHEN MOVING

While your car's twelve-volt outlet (the "cigarette lighter") may work when the engine is off, anything plugged in and drawing power when the car isn't running will eventually drain your battery. This is because the car's alternator—the device that charges the battery and creates current for other electronics—operates only when the engine is running.

DON'T DRIVE JUST TO CHARGE SOMETHING

Obviously, driving consumes fuel, and gasoline costs more (and pollutes more) than electrical power. Don't drive aimlessly for three hours to recharge the iPod that you could just plug into a wall socket (or your computer). But if you're going to be driving anyway, it makes sense to use the alternator to charge electronics.

CHARGE THINGS WITH SMALL BATTERIES

Cell phones, PDAs, and music players have small, efficient batteries that charge quickly. They're also more likely to have "intelligent" batteries that speed-charge to nearly full capacity, as well as circuitry to prevent overcharging. That thousand-candlepower emergency searchlight with a two-pound battery may take twelve hours to charge in a car but just half that time plugged into the wall.

CHOOSE THE RIGHT GEAR

You can find dozens of power-thirsty appliances that can be run from your car, from televisions to camping refrigerators. But these are typically items that plug in and draw power continuously—and don't have rechargeable batteries. Instead, consider such items as small coffeepots, electric shavers, cameras, battery-powered lanterns, and the like. These either have batteries that can be recharged or are designed to operate for short periods on a charge, instead of needing to stay plugged in all the time.

RECHARGE RECHARGEABLES

One of the best uses of your car's alternator is to recharge rechargeable batteries that can then be used to power any number of devices. Many high-quality battery chargers even include car adapters. Just make sure your ride is long enough to give them a full charge.

USE A MULTIFUNCTION CHARGER

You can also use your car to charge small electronics (phones, PDAs, game players) through their USB ports rather than their power sockets, which may be proprietary. Amazon sells a number of inexpensive (less than $20) devices; search for "universal USB car charger." Most of these chargers include a number of adaptors to fit various types of electronics, which means you'll (hopefully) only need to buy one.

BUY MULTIFUNCTION APPLIANCES

If you're buying a gadget that allows you to, say, listen to your iPod through your car's speakers, make sure it also recharges the iPod at the same time. It may cost a little more initially, but it will save electricity in the long run.

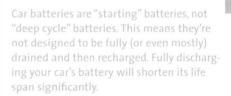

Car batteries are "starting" batteries, not "deep cycle" batteries. This means they're not designed to be fully (or even mostly) drained and then recharged. Fully discharging your car's battery will shorten its life span significantly.

CHAPTER 9

THE ROOF
Sun, Wind, and Rain Power

For the truly green home, a roof is like a candy store: lots of ways to spend money, but best not to go overboard. This chapter's projects cover everything: green roofs, rainwater collection, wind turbines, and energy-efficient chimneys and attics. You probably won't tackle them all at once—and, in truth, you probably won't be able to afford more than a few, at least until prices come down. But it's best to think of these projects as large investments that pay an annual return, in the form of savings, rather than as technologies that will completely pay for themselves over a set number of years. So grab your hammer and a ladder and read on.

CONSTRUCT A GREEN ROOF

Our ancestors discovered the benefits of living below sod long ago. Homes set into hillsides ("soddies") were warmer in winter, cooler in summer, and their roofs weren't exposed to the elements, which made them last longer. Today's modern green roofs offer the same advantages, plus a number of new ones. They reduce storm water runoff, lower utility bills, muffle sound, and absorb CO_2 and release oxygen. And they look awesome. You'll want a professional to help you install yours, but the basic concept and directions are easy to understand.

MATERIALS	$15 per square foot and up

- ☐ Roof of appropriate slope (between 5 and 20 degrees is ideal, though a flat roof will work)
- ☐ Sub-membrane material
- ☐ Waterproofing material
- ☐ Water retention mat
- ☐ Drainage/soil filter mat
- ☐ Soil mix/growth substrate
- ☐ Plants (typically, some drought-tolerant species of sedum or grasses or mosses, depending on the climate)

STEPS TO CONSTRUCT THE ROOF

1. Determine roof slope. Roofs with a slight incline are good candidates for greening because gravity will drain water naturally, eliminating the need for a built-up structure to angle plants and hold them in place. However, since most green roofs are generally not intended for pedestrians, slopes of up to 40 degrees may be used, with the necessary framing and support.

2. Certify the roof's load-bearing capacity. A fully saturated green roof will add a minimum of 20 pounds per square foot of additional weight to the existing roof structure. Thus, you'll need a structural engineer to examine the roof and its joists to make sure it can support the added load without major (read: pricey) modifications.

3. Add drainage. The lowest edge of the roof should have a gutter that collects runoff and connects to a downspout that runs to a storm sewer (or rain barrel; see "Capture and Reuse Rainwater," page 154).

4. Waterproof the roof. A green roof is like a layer cake, with each layer a critical piece of the whole. The bottom layer is the waterproof membrane, which sits on top of the existing roof and is typically installed by a roofer. If it fails, you're in for trouble.

5. Apply the water/soil retention and drainage layers. These two layers keep the plants sufficiently irrigated, hold them in place and prevent erosion, and filter excess water down

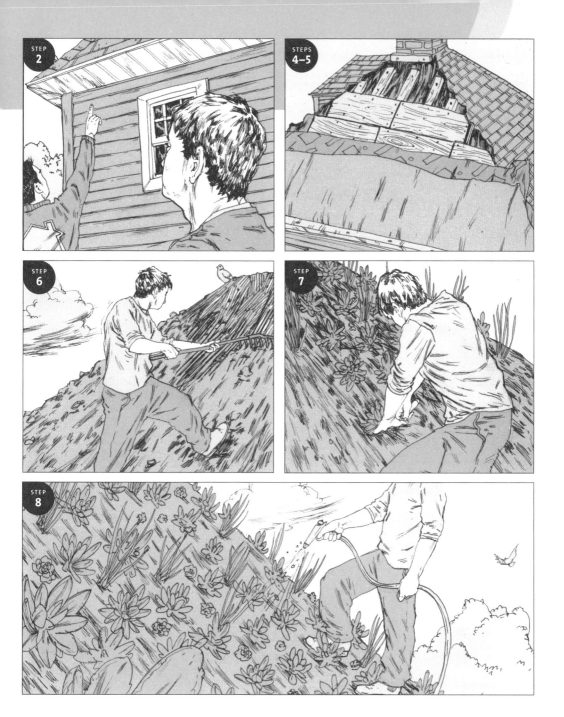

and away from fully saturated plants. The materials used will depend on the climate and plants, but they may include clay, pumice, florist foam, spray mulch, and various polymers.

6. Add the growth substrate. The precise soil mixture will depend on the climate, plants, and roof structure. All-natural soil isn't used on green roofs because of its weight and tendency to compact. Instead, you'll use a mix of organic and inorganic matter that's lightweight and has good water retention.

7. Add plants. Planting a green roof isn't as simple as rolling out some sod. Plants are added in "plugs" and spaced carefully.

8. Water. Most green roofs don't require special irrigation (or cutting or mowing, for that matter). However, to establish plants in very hot climates and during the first six months or so, the roof should be watered if there isn't sufficient rainfall.

9. Fertilize (optional). In most cases, fertilization probably won't be necessary. However, for very large roofs an application of slow-release fertilizer may be necessary once a year.

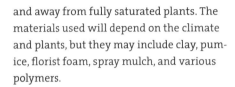

- Ford Motor Company's assembly plant in Dearborn, Michigan, has a green roof that's more than ten acres.

- A carefully designed green roof can be used recreationally—mostly for sitting or strolling, not playing football.

- Green roofs aren't perfect. Although leaks are rare, they're not unheard of, and locating and fixing one can be more difficult than repairing a standard roof.

- Owing to their specialized installation requirements, green roofs can cost 30 to 60 percent more to install per square foot than standard roofs (though costs have come down considerably over the past few years). However, grants from the EPA's Clean Water Program are available. Assume a minimum of $15 per square foot, not including waterproofing. Utility savings should make up for added cost.

- Most green roofs are guaranteed for decades longer than standard roofs.

- Green roof owners may receive a credit instead of a bill from their local water utility if the company charges for storm water runoff, as many are beginning to do.

- Some 1.5 square meters (16.15 square feet) of uncut grass produces enough oxygen annually to supply one person's yearly oxygen intake requirement.

MAKE YOUR STANDARD ROOF MORE ENERGY EFFICIENT

If a green roof isn't practical or affordable, you can still take some steps to make your plain old ordinary roof more efficient. The exact methods and costs will vary based on roof construction and slope, materials, and age, but the following general tips are inexpensive and will pay for themselves over time.

CHECK GUTTERS TWICE YEARLY

Clean out debris and make sure that runoff is draining properly. Standing water on your roof will eventually cause leaks, and blocked gutters force water over the side of your home, where it can cause rot. Trim trees around the roofline to prevent new clogs and to keep destructive animals such as squirrels off your roof.

CHECK FOR ICE DAMS IN WINTER

Ice dams on your roof are an indicator of heat escaping from the attic or top floor, typically through cracks in areas with poor insulation. Consider adding insulation, or at the very least caulking any obvious openings. An attic fan can also reduce ice damming in winter.

SILVER-COAT

Flat roofs that aren't pebbled should be silver-coated to reflect sunlight and lower the internal temperature of your home—particularly the top floor. If you have a roof-mounted central air conditioner, rust-proof and then silver-coat all exposed ductwork to keep the air inside cold. All exterior ductwork should be insulated.

ADD AN ATTIC VENT

A wind-driven attic vent pulls hot air out of your home without using electricity, which can lower your utility bills. Even for homes without an attic, a roof vent can help cool the crawl space below joists.

INSULATE

Older homes may not be well insulated below the roof. Use blow-in insulation to help regulate temperature.

CAP CHIMNEYS

Chimneys for fireplaces, furnaces, gas hot water heaters, and plumbing stacks should be capped to keep rain and animals out of your home and reduce downdrafts. You can also improve the efficiency of your fireplace by adding a draft cap, which will increase airflow.

If you have a flat roof, consider placing your central air-conditioning unit on it, instead of on the ground; it costs a little more during installation, but it's worth it. Because warm air rises and cooled air falls, the system won't have to work as hard to cool the top (hottest) floor of your home—which means you can keep the thermostat set a little higher, saving electricity.

INSTALL SOLAR PANELS

Perhaps no other power-generating technology holds the promise of solar (aka photo-voltaic, or "PV") energy. Sunlight costs nothing; it's safe; it's extraction-, waste-, and emissions-free; and it's infinitely renewable—at least until the sun supernovas in a billion years or so. As with fossil fuels, though, there are costs associated with capturing solar radiation and converting it into electricity. The problem has been—and remains—that on a kilowatt-per-hour basis, solar power is more expensive than its polluting competition. Nevertheless, adding a photovoltaic array to your house will sharply reduce your carbon footprint and, depending on where you live, might even save you money. For a truly green home, it's a bright idea.

MATERIALS	$20,000 installed, for an average-size system

- ☐ Photovoltaic array (1.2–5 kilowatts total for an average home
- ☐ Power inverter
- ☐ Roof mounts with stainless steel lag bolts
- ☐ Flashing
- ☐ Metal rails (to connect mounts)
- ☐ Roofing tar
- ☐ Reflective roof coating, roof cement, hot tar
- ☐ Stud finder
- ☐ Drill

- You can determine local renewable energy incentives by visiting www.dsire usa.org/index.cfm.

- Visit www.solarhome.org for a list of PV retailers.

STEPS TO INSTALL THE PANELS

1. Attach the mounts to the roof. The mounts for the PV array must be secured to roof joists; use the stud finder to locate them. (The best time to install a rooftop solar array is when you're redoing the roof anyway.) Drill into the joists using a pilot bit to prevent splitting, secure the mounts with lag bolts, then secure them with roofing cement. The mounts must be in two straight lines, one a few feet in front of the other. The two lines may be at slightly different heights to angle the panels, depending on the home's orientation and geographic location relative to the equator.

2. Install flashing. This will help to prevent leaks around the roof penetrations. Secure it with roof cement, then hot-mop it with tar.

3. Install the rails. They will support the PV panels. They should be connected to the roof mounts with stainless steel bolts.

4. Install the PV panels. Typical glass-coated PV panels (or "modules") will be installed in sets of two or three to form an array or series; the number will depend on the kilowatt rating of the modules, the available square footage, and the home's energy needs (see Carbon Counter, right). Attach them to the rails with their included hardware.

5. Connect the array to the power inverter via a conduit, then connect the conduit to the power line. Because PV arrays produce direct current (DC), they require an inverter module to change that to alternating current (AC), which is typical household current. Unless this all sounds familiar, hire an electrician for this step.

6. Contact your electric utility. Houses that are "off the grid" may store electricity in a large lead-acid battery array for later use. In most installations, though, PV arrays are "grid-tiered": The electricity will go either directly into the home to meet its energy needs or upstream, back into the power grid. During periods of peak electricity demand, you'll essentially be "selling" your power back to the utility in the form of a credit. This will lower your electric bill.

- How long will it take for a PV array to pay for itself in energy savings? It's a fair question, and one that most green homeowners will consider before making the investment—especially since a high-efficiency residential PV array can cost tens of thousands of dollars. There are a number of factors to consider when making a decision. These include available federal and state tax credits and local utility grants, your home's annual energy needs, utility rates, the amount of direct sunlight where you live, and the available square footage. Most systems will more than pay for themselves over their expected lifetimes—and in some cases in just a few years. Figure a 10–15 percent return per annum. Visit www.ameco solar.com/PVWHAT03.html for details.

- A high-efficiency solar array will produce one kilowatt per hour for every one hundred square feet used; the smallest systems are fifty square feet (five by ten feet).

- A two-kilowatt system can cost $20,000, before credits. The cost per watt decreases as the array gets larger, so a five-kilowatt system may cost $35,000.

- Typical residential PV systems have a peak power production of between 1,200 and five thousand watts, requiring anywhere from 150 to more than one thousand square feet of installed area, depending on the efficiency of the PV technology.

CAPTURE AND REUSE RAINWATER

A modern rain barrel is one of the easiest—and cheapest—ways to reduce your home's water demands. Studies have shown that in the United States, lawn and garden watering make up about 40 percent of total household water usage in summer. You can capture virtually all the water that would otherwise go down your storm drain with a minimal investment and an hour's work.

MATERIALS	$25

- ☐ 55-gallon plastic drum (available at home-improvement and garden stores)
- ☐ Saber or keyhole saw
- ☐ Two small hinges, with screws
- ☐ 3/4-inch galvanized coupling
- ☐ 3/4-inch galvanized nipple
- ☐ 3/4-inch galvanized flange sill faucet
- ☐ One 1 1/2-inch stop screw
- ☐ Hose
- ☐ Caulk
- ☐ Drill with 3/8-inch bit
- ☐ Screwdriver
- ☐ Household cleaner and sponge
- ☐ Pencil
- ☐ Wire mesh (optional, for reducing clogs)

- Rainwater from your roof isn't safe for humans or pets to drink.

- Place your barrel on a raised platform to create more water pressure.

- If you plan to use your rain barrel for lawn watering, consider installing a screen or mesh filter near the top of the barrel to keep leaf litter out of the hose.

- Mosquitoes breed in standing water, so remember to actually use the water in your rain barrel within a day or so.

STEPS TO REUSE RAINWATER

1. Drill a small hole through the top of the barrel, 1 inch inside the rim. Use the saw to cut a hole large enough to accept your downspout, typically about 4 inches in diameter. (You may need to widen an existing opening.)

2. Draw a line across the top of the barrel from one side to the other, a few inches off center. Drill a hole at one end, then use the saw to cut across the barrel. Continue to saw around the edge of the barrel (on the opposite side of the downspout hole) until you can remove this semicircular section. (Premade rain barrels may already have this section hinged.) Drill holes for the hinges, then screw them into the top of the barrel, along the straight edge, so the removed section can be swung up to remove debris from the barrel. Install a stop, using a screw, to prevent the lid from swinging into the barrel.

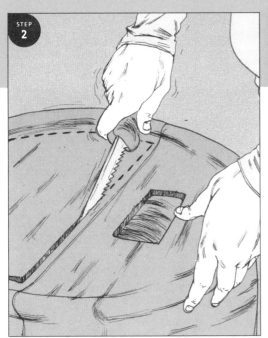

3. Cut a 1-inch-diameter hole near the bottom of the barrel. Hold the coupling on the inside of the barrel while you thread the nipple through the hole into it. Screw the flange of the faucet into the nipple on the outside of the barrel. Caulk. Connect the hose to the faucet.

4. Clean out the barrel, using a household cleaner. Although rainwater should never be used for drinking—after all, it flowed across your roof—it's still a good idea to remove any residual chemicals from the barrel.

5. Place the barrel on bricks, then place your downspout through the receiver hole you made in Step 1. Use the hose to remove the rainwater for watering plants and lawn. Consider adding an overflow cutout with an attached piece of drainpipe near the top of the barrel. This pipe can lead to a second rain barrel to handle overflow, or it can send excess water away from the side of your house.

- The EPA estimates that a single rain barrel can save most homeowners almost thirteen hundred gallons of water—just in summer! However, a typical lawn requires three thousand gallons of water. Per month.

- A rain barrel does more than save you money on your water bill. It also reduces storm runoff, which in turn can eliminate the need for newer and more expensive water treatment facilities—facilities you pay for with your taxes.

INSTALL A WIND TURBINE

Unlike PV arrays, wind turbines (aka "wind generators") have proven difficult—in many cases, impossible—to install in residential settings. Usually this is due to their height: To harness steady wind, such turbines must be above surrounding trees and buildings and thus can reach eighty feet high, violating zoning restrictions in most highly populated areas. Wind farms have also encountered strong opposition from animal rights activists—because their spinning blades can injure birds—and from some environmentalists, because they may obstruct scenic vistas. But new "compact" and "micro-mini" turbines are smaller, lighter, and cheaper, and they may be just the ticket for a green home.

MATERIALS	$500–$5,000

- ☐ Compact wind turbine or micro-mini turbine array
- ☐ Inverter (may be built-in, depending on model)
- ☐ Battery array (optional)
- ☐ Unobstructed windy location (10 mph minimum; see Green Bits, next page, for a wind map link)

For a typical home that uses about 9,400 kilowatt-hours per year, a wind turbine rated from 5 to 15 kilowatt-hours will meet most of the home's electricity needs.

STEPS TO INSTALL THE TURBINE

1. Determine available space. Even a relatively low compact turbine may have a 12-foot rotor and a 30-foot tower—not exactly ideal for a one-bedroom condo, even one with a balcony. However, if you live in a low-density area with steady wind, and can obtain the necessary permits, this is the way to go. These turbines cost about $5,000 and can produce 5–15 kilowatts per month at wind speeds of 12 mph (5.4 meters per second), covering anywhere from 30 to 80 percent of the typical home's electricity needs. If you've got lots of room for one of these turbines, skip to Step 4. If you live in a city or a typical suburban development, continue to Step 2.

2. Monitor wind speed. If your home is in an area where a large rotary-type turbine isn't practical, you may still be able to use a micro-mini turbine array. These turbines look like a series of small fans (or, in some cases, gears), each about 10 inches in diameter. Set in a row, they can take up as little as 15 feet of space; multiple rows can also be linked. With a steady breeze, twenty micro-mini turbines can generate 4 kilowatt-hours per day, or 120 per month. (The average U.S. home uses about 780 kilowatt-hours per month.) This is clearly a small contribution—particularly

in comparison to a tall turbine that can cover nearly all of the home's energy needs—but the initial investment is less than $1,000, and it will pay for itself quickly.

3. Install the array. Micro-mini turbines are set in a small frame and attached to an inverter and, typically, a battery. Setup is straightforward and takes less than an hour—though you may want an electrician for the final connections.

4. Site the tower and apply for permits. Although they can be installed by homeowners, rotary-type turbines must be placed atop high towers, and the rotor must be at least 20 feet above nearby trees and structures, which makes installation more complicated. (As a general rule, the higher the turbine, the more power it's able to generate. But the height of your tower will probably be governed by zoning restrictions.) Most wind turbine manufacturers recommend the use of a professional engineer for safe and effective installation—and they don't recommend installing a rotary turbine on the roof.

5. Connect it to power lines or a battery array. Rotary turbines create enough electricity to sell some back to the local utility, as with photovoltaic arrays, if desired. Whether or not you do will depend on your energy needs and/or your desire for the added cost of a battery array to store excess power.

- The U.S. government provides wind power resources and wind maps to help you determine if your home's location is windy enough for a turbine. For details visit www.eere.energy.gov/windandhydro/windpoweringamerica/wind_maps.asp.

- A fairly new tool known as a hand winch or scaffold winch can, in some circumstances, eliminate the need for costly and cumbersome electrical hoists when erecting wind turbine towers.

- Skystream (www.skystreamenergy.com) manufactures a number of residential wind turbines that are in widespread use, mostly in the West and Southwest.

- The Motorwave Group (www.motorwave group.com) manufactures the Motorwave, a micro-mini turbine array for commercial and residential applications where tower-based rotors aren't feasible.

- The Scottish company Windsave (www.windsave.com) sells what it terms a "rooftop" wind turbine that can be pole-mounted at a height of about ten feet. It costs about $4,000 installed, but it cannot be self-installed and is currently not available outside the United Kingdom.

STEP 1

STEP 2

STEP 3

STEP 5

RECYCLE PRETTY MUCH ALL THE OLD JUNK IN YOUR ATTIC

The best way to get rid of stuff you're not using is, of course, to sell it or give it to someone who can use it—and keep it out of a landfill. But realistically, most of us have boxes and cartons and trunks of decades-old junk that we figure nobody in his or her right mind would want. That's where the Web comes in. Sites such as craigslist (www.craigslist.org) and eBay (www.ebay.com) are great if you want to try to make some money—though eBay, at least, has a fairly steep learning curve. The Freecycle Network (www.freecycle.org) is dedicated to removing things from the waste stream and is another good choice. But there are also a number of specialized sites and organizations that are probably a better bet for particular kinds of objects. These are listed below.

OLD BOOKS

Amazon is the eight-hundred-pound gorilla of the used book market, but there's also Book-Mooch (www.bookmooch.com), where you can list the books you have and receive "points" for giving them away; the points can then be used to get books you actually want to read. And if cataloging your hundreds of dusty volumes doesn't sound appealing, you can always cart them to a local used bookstore.

CLOTHING

This one's easy. The Salvation Army (www.salvationarmyusa.org) or any other qualified charity will take almost any piece of clothing, except underwear. There are also specialized organizations for prom and formal dresses (www.donatemydress.org, www.glassslipperproject.org) and business attire (www.enchantedcloset.org).

HARDWARE, FURNITURE, WINDOWS, FLOORING

Second Chance Inc. (www.secondchanceinc.org) will pick up virtually any reusable building element in the Mid-Atlantic region, for free, and recondition it for reuse. It also has a job training program for low-income residents of Baltimore, Philadelphia, and Washington, D.C., which teaches skills in everything from carpentry to craftsmanship.

OLD SNEAKERS

Nike's "Reuse-A-Shoe" Program (www.nikereuseashoe.com) recycles old sneakers (any brand) into rubber-based sports surfaces. Sneakers can be dropped off at various locations; the Web site has a list. Sneakers—and shoes—that have been lightly worn can be sent to Shoe4Africa (www.shoe4africa.org), or donors can mail them directly to Kenya, where they're distributed (see the Web site).

COMPUTERS AND ELECTRONICS

Who doesn't have an attic (or basement, or closet) filled with "technotrash"? Much of this stuff is manufactured with heavy metals that should not go into a landfill. Recycles.org (www.recycles.org) matches donors and recipients, and it specializes in computer and office equipment. Share the Technology (www.sharetechnology.org) offers a similar service, and it also has a database of computer recycling organizations throughout the country. The Wireless Foundation (www.wirelessfoundation.org) collects and recycles cell phones (as does Whole Foods). Educational Assistance Limited (www.inventorydonations.org) actually turns electronics into college financial assistance for needy students.

TAPES AND DVDS

So-called e-waste probably fills a few boxes in your home. GreenDisk (www.greendisk.com) will recycle old cassettes, videocassettes, jewel cases, CDs, DVDs, and even printer cartridges.

OLD EYEGLASSES

These can be dropped off at any LensCrafters, Pearle Vision, Sears Optical, Target Optical, or Sunglass Hut location, where they will go to the Give the Gift of Sight Foundation (www.givethegiftofsight.com).

KITCHEN AND BATHROOM WARE

Although they won't take your old utensils, the company Recycline (www.recycline.com) makes the Preserve brand of home products, which are made from recycled materials—in some cases, Stonyfield Farm yogurt containers—and which it will also recycle for you if you send them back, for free. (The old plastic is used to make plastic lumber for benches and decks.) Or you can drop them in any #5 recycling container. Their products are available at Target, Trader Joe's, and Whole Foods.

PRETTY MUCH ANYTHING ELSE

The Web site Earth 911 (www.earth911.org) is an excellent resource for recycling just about anything, and also has good energy-saving tips.

CHAPTER 10

THE YARD
Sustainable Agriculture and Aquaculture

An eco-house need not be a green hovel; you can still keep your lawn and your pool. (Although the old maxim still holds true: It's better to know someone with a pool than to own one yourself.) Nevertheless, there are a number of outdoor projects that can reduce your emissions, lower your bills, and assuage your guilt about having bought the biggest piece of the American dream you could possibly afford. This chapter's projects run the green gamut, from building a composter to making natural pesticides to constructing a bat house. Oh, and raising rainbow trout in your pool. You can swim in your neighbor's, right?.

BUILD A COMPOSTER

A composter isn't exactly emissions-free: After all, decaying organic matter emits CO_2 into the atmosphere. But the composting process repurposes household waste, which otherwise would have to be transported and buried, or burned. And it turns trash into chemical-free fertilizer using sun, air, and rain. These benefits alone outweigh the virtually imperceptible emissions from your compost pile.

MATERIALS	$50

- ☐ Wood pallet
- ☐ Four 5-foot wood posts
- ☐ Four sections of steel mesh (chicken wire), 3 square feet each
- ☐ Staple gun, or wire and pliers for cutting
- ☐ Pitchfork
- ☐ Shovel
- ☐ Soil
- ☐ Mower (for leaves and lawn clippings)
- ☐ Knife or food processor (for chopping kitchen waste)
- ☐ Composting material (see Step 5)

You can purchase a premade composting bin for about $100 or fancier, self-contained composting systems for $500 and up. The latter, sometimes called "kitchen composters," are typically fairly small and require electricity for venting, as well as the regular addition of items such as sawdust and baking soda. And, of course, you still need a yard in which to use all that compost. On the plus side, these machines can (in theory) accept cooked food items, be used inside, and operate during winter months when outdoor composters are dormant. (See www.naturemill.com for an example of a kitchen composter.)

STEPS TO BUILD THE COMPOSTER

1. Determine position of the compost pile. The composter should get a reasonable amount of sunlight (half a day) and should remain damp. However, it should not be allowed to dry out or become oversaturated. Make sure there are several feet of space on each side for proper aeration.

2. Place pallet on the ground. The pallet will keep the bottom of the pile from becoming too wet, and it will allow air to circulate beneath it.

3. Position posts. Using the shovel, dig holes for the posts and set one at each corner of the pallet. They should be buried at least 6 inches; 1 foot is better.

4. Attach the mesh to the posts using staples or wire to make an open box with the pallet as the base.

5. The composter should be filled in layers in the following order, bottom to top: layer 1: organic material (6–8 inches; see Green Bits, right); layer 2: fertilizer (commercial, or 2 inches of animal manure); layer 3: topsoil (1 or 2 inches; avoid soils with insecticides). Repeat the layering, moving upward, two or three more times until the bin is full.

6. Allow time for heating. Natural decomposition occurs best in the 110–160°F range. During late spring to summer, the pile should reach this range naturally in about two weeks: When you see the pile settle, you'll know the process is working.

7. Turn the pile and water it. If you don't add new organic material, turn the pile to aerate it about once a month. Add water if the pile isn't damp to the touch. (If it begins to have an unpleasant odor, it's probably too wet; aerate it more often and/or cover it with a tarp.) If you add new material, turn it once every two weeks.

8. Examine the compost. When it's dark brown and crumbly, with an earthen texture, it's almost ready for use. None of the original material should be recognizable, except for some small wood chips.

9. Remove the compost and allow it to sit for two weeks to stabilize and cool.

10. Use it. When produced correctly, compost helps the soil retain nutrients, moisture, and air, and it helps plants and vegetables grow quickly.

More than ninety-six billion pounds of edible food are wasted each year in the United States—including 122 pounds, each month, for a family of four.

- Good potential choices for household organic waste: peels, rinds, and cores from fruits and vegetables; coffee grounds and tea leaves; crushed egg and peanut shells; vegetable scraps; and some nonrecyclable paper.

- Choices to avoid: meat and fish scraps (they attract rodents and cause odors); dairy; limes; walnut and pecan shells; corncobs (unless chopped or shredded); peat moss; plants and clippings treated with insecticide; glossy paper from magazines; human and pet waste.

- Organic material used in a compost pile should be cut into small pieces to accelerate the decomposition process. Use a mower to chop leaves and grass, and a kitchen knife or food processor to finely chop household waste. Use a paper shredder for paper, or tear it into tiny scraps.

- The presence and location of backyard composters may be controlled by zoning laws in some places; check local regulations.

USES FOR FLIES AND WORMS

You may find that your backyard composter attracts insects—particularly flies—and is invaded by worms. Rather than think of these as problem pests, consider the following uses for them.

PET FOOD

Flies are an excellent food source for pet frogs, lizards, and fish. You can trap them alive, using store-bought bottle-type fly traps, or you can easily make one of these traps yourself. Drop a small piece of raw meat into an empty plastic soda bottle, then tape a plastic funnel with a one-quarter-inch neck into the neck of the soda bottle, wide end facing up: Flies crawl in but can't get out. Place the trap in the freezer for two minutes to slow the flies down, then remove the funnel, shake a few out, and place them in the pet's terrarium. As they warm up, they'll begin moving again.

VERMICOMPOST

Worms that appear in your compost pile can themselves be combined with other compostable food scraps, soil, and wet, shredded newspaper to make a nutrient-rich compost called vermi-compost, or worm castings. Just drill some drain holes in the bottom of a plastic container about eight inches deep, add the materials above, and then add about one pound of worms and replace the lid. (Note that the worms found in a compost pile, called "red worms" or "red wigglers," aren't the same as plain old earthworms; they eat more and reproduce more quickly, making them more suitable for vermiculture.) Harvest the compost in three to six months.

VENUS FLYTRAP FOOD

Venus flytraps (*Dionaea muscipula*) are insectivorous plants that attract and kill flies, from which they derive their nutrients. Put a few outside and watch the action as the flies land, touch the plant's trigger hairs, and get devoured as the trap snaps shut. They require moist soil and a warm, humid environment, higher than 70°F at all times. Water them only with distilled or rain water, as chlorine and other chemicals in tap water can be harmful. Ideally, the plants should be in a terrarium, but they may be grown in plastic containers with sides as high as the top of the plant. You can feed the plants flies that have died of natural causes—wriggle them around to force the trap to shut—but don't feed them hamburger, Kobe beef, or shoofly pie.

AQUARIUM FISH FOOD

Most aquarium fish more than four inches long will eat earthworms. Rinse the worms in clean water, then cut them into small pieces before feeding the fish. The worms may also be placed in freezer bags and frozen.

BAIT

Red worms typically will stay alive, hooked and underwater, for at least thirty minutes, making them an excellent choice for attracting fish, especially bass, perch, and bream.

BUILD A BAT HOUSE

Bats are one of nature's best forms of insect control. A single bat can eat up to two thousand insects an hour, and tens of millions over its lifetime. A bat will eat anything that flies—especially mosquitoes, which are active at dusk, the time when most bats begin feeding. They're also sociable animals that prefer to live with other bats, so a well-constructed bat house will probably attract a number of bats.

MATERIALS	$40

- □ 1/4 sheet (2 x 4 feet) of 1/2-inch non-pressure-treated plywood.
- □ One piece of 1 inch x 2 inch x 8 foot pine (spacer strip)
- □ One board, 1 x 3 x 28 inches (roof)
- □ Twelve 1 1/2-inch outdoor screws
- □ Two 32-inch nails (for mounting)
- □ 1 pint dark exterior wood stain
- □ 1 pint dark exterior primer
- □ 1 pint exterior black paint
- □ Caulk
- □ Saw (table or circular recommended)
- □ Drill
- □ Screwdriver
- □ Paintbrushes
- □ Plastic mesh (optional)

You can purchase a premade bat house online. These range in size and price, though even the smallest ones are typically more than $100—more than twice the cost of the materials needed to build one yourself.

STEPS TO BUILD THE BAT HOUSE

1. Measure and cut the plywood into three pieces: 26 1/2 x 24 inches (back), 16 1/2 x 24 inches (upper front), and 5 x 24 inches (lower front). Measure and cut the trim strip into one 24-inch and two 20 1/2-inch pieces.

2. Roughen the inside surfaces of the boards by cutting 1/16-inch-deep grooves across them, 1/2-inch apart. Optionally, staple plastic mesh to the pieces in place of the grooves. The grooves or mesh provides the bats with something to cling to as they enter and inhabit the house. (If using mesh, perform Steps 3–4 first, then attach the mesh and continue with Step 5.)

3. Stain all wood pieces on both sides and allow them to dry overnight. Don't allow stain to fill the grooves. Repeat for a second coat.

4. Prime and paint all exterior surfaces. Don't use oil-based primer or paint. Use dark-colored primer and paint.

5. Drill two holes near the top of the back section, for hanging the bat house.

6. Assemble the bat house. Attach trim strips to the back with screws, starting with the 24-inch piece at top. The interior will be 3/4 inch wide (front to back). Caulk. Attach the front to spacer strips with screws, the upper piece first. Caulk, then attach the lower section. Leave 1/2 inch of vent space between the upper and lower front pieces.

7. Attach the 1-x-3-x-28-inch board to the top as a roof. Caulk all seams.

8. Using long nails, mount the bat house at least 15 feet off the ground in a southeast-facing, sunny spot, preferably on the side of a structure or on a pole, not in a tree (to keep it away from predators). It should be close to a stream or other water source.

- Bat guano is an excellent fertilizer.

- Bats prefer warmer temperatures in their roosting places, 80–100°F. Consider adding some insulation just below the roof of your bat house, to retain heat.

- Bats can carry rabies, and in the United States bats are the most common source of human rabies. However, your chances of acquiring the disease from any source are minuscule: There are only one or two documented cases per year, on average.

- What are your chances of actually getting bats to live in your bat house? Pretty good. Studies indicate that well-made, correctly positioned bat houses are populated about 60 percent of the time, on average, and 90 percent of those were populated within two years of being constructed. Note, however, that you cannot bait a bat house; the bats must discover it on their own.

ZERO-EMISSIONS WORKOUT: PUSH MOWER—BASED EXERCISES

5 BODY BOOSTS

A green house really shouldn't have a lush green lawn: Lawns account for billions of gallons of water usage and millions of tons of emissions from gas-powered mowers each year (not to mention ridiculous amounts of pesticides). If you're not willing to replace your real grass with the artificial variety, at least try using a push mower to eliminate your emissions from cutting it. Once you've made the switch, consider performing the following exercises to make manual mowing (even more of) a workout. Note: You won't burn calories if your landscaper mows for you.

THE "JOG" MOW

Instead of walking behind the mower, increase your pace so you're jogging slowly. This exercise works best with lightweight aluminum mowers. Consider challenging a neighbor to a short "mower race" on your lawn for faster results.

MUSCLES WORKED

- ☐ heart
- ☐ arms
- ☐ legs

170

THE "LUNGE" MOW

Place the mower in front of you, feet slightly apart, hands on the push bar. Push the mower and simultaneously move your right foot forward and bend your right knee, while keeping your left foot planted. Place your right foot on the ground ahead of you and shift your weight from the ball of your left foot to your right foot, then hold in this position for two seconds. Pull the mower back as you bring your right foot back and place your feet in the starting position again. Repeat with your left leg, then move to a new patch of grass and repeat.

MUSCLES WORKED

☐ quads

THE "PUSH-PULL" MOW

Place the mower in front of you, hands on the handle and arms slightly bent. Keeping your back straight and feet planted, push the mower ahead of you by straightening your arms, then pull it back to its starting position. Move to a new section of grass and repeat.

MUSCLES WORKED

- ☐ biceps
- ☐ triceps
- ☐ anterior

THE "CALF RAISE" MOW

Position the mower in front of you. Place your hands on the push bar. Grip it tightly. Now, gently rock forward onto the balls of your feet as you simultaneously lift up on the push bar, raising the mower slightly as if it were a barbell. Hold for three counts, then relax. Push the mower forward to cut some grass, then repeat for three sets of ten raises, moving to a new section of lawn after each raise. This exercise works best with old-style cast iron mowers.

MUSCLES WORKED

- ☐ gastrocnemius
- ☐ soleus

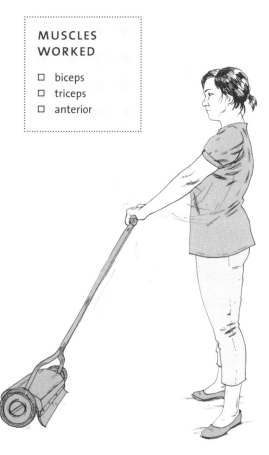

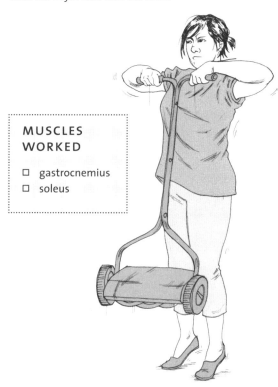

THE "STARTER PULL" MOW (GAS-POWERED MOWERS, ZERO EMISSIONS)

The mower should be unprimed or empty of fuel. Stand next to the mower on the side with the starter cable, facing forward. Reach across your body and grasp the cable firmly. Pull it to its full extension, then release it. Repeat for twelve pulls. Turn around and face the other direction, then repeat with the other arm. Repeat for two more sets.

Note: This exercise won't trim the grass.

MUSCLES WORKED

- ☐ forearms
- ☐ biceps
- ☐ triceps
- ☐ anterior deltoids

173

BUILD AND STOCK A FISHPOND

The environmental benefits of a backyard fishpond are numerous: Fish eat mosquitoes and other pests, you'll have less grass to mow, water absorbs sunlight to keep your backyard cooler, and the trickle of water is relaxing. And, of course, fish can be eaten. Another benefit: Fish will reproduce at no cost. Just don't eat too many at once, or you'll empty the gene pool.

MATERIALS	$500, depending on size, layout, and depth

- ☐ Shovel
- ☐ Edger
- ☐ Spray paint or string
- ☐ Pond underlay
- ☐ Waterproof pond liner (rubber for a large pond, precast vinyl for a smaller one)
- ☐ Pond filter (intake)
- ☐ Pond waterfall (output)
- ☐ Rocks and gravel
- ☐ Plants
- ☐ Fish
- ☐ Hose and water source
- ☐ Outdoor extension cord
- ☐ Scissors or utility knife
- ☐ Sump pump

STEPS TO BUILD THE POND

1. Mark the pond's boundary. A fishpond can be any shape or size. Based on the available land, mark the boundary of the pond using string or spray paint. If using a premade vinyl liner, trace around it.

2. Using the edger, dig around the marked perimeter of your pond, then dig the pond out with the shovel. The pond interior may be stepped, with the center deeper than the edges. One section of the pond should be at least 7 feet deep if you live in a cold climate and you want your fish to overwinter.

3. Position filter and waterfall. The filter should be buried near one side of the pond, not in the middle. Mark its location with paint or string, then dig to the depth indicated on its instructions. The waterfall (or other ornamental output) should be on the opposite side of the pond. You can connect the two by digging a ditch, which will also make a small ornamental stream.

4. Position the underlay in the pond, smoothing out wrinkles. This layer will prevent rocks and debris from puncturing the waterproof liner, which should be placed on top. Cut it to fit.

5. Position rocks. Large rocks should line the perimeter and each layer of the pond, to prevent slippage of the liners. The rocks should be sizable—1–2 feet in diameter—and placed close together.

6. Add gravel. Pour the gravel into all gaps among the rocks, as well as onto any exposed liner surface.

7. Wash the rocks. Using the hose, wash dirt and debris from the rocks, then pump out the dirty water with the sump pump.

8. Add aquatic plants.

9. Add water. Submerge the filter completely.

10. Add fish. Keep them in their plastic bags and leave the bags in the water for a few hours to allow the fish to acclimate, as you would for fish in a fish tank. Then release the fish. Typically, koi and other ornamental fish are used in backyard fishponds. (See Green Bits, below, for more edible choices.)

- Provided that the water is kept cool, you can stock a large pond with any number of edible species, including trout, carp, perch, tilapia, catfish, and even smallmouth bass. (Catching them requires nothing more than a net, though you can always use a deck chair and a rod and reel for more of a challenge.) The rub is that most nontropical edible species prefer cold water, and the flesh may turn mushy in a warmer pond without rapidly moving water. If you do decide to raise fish for cooking, consider adding a second large output device, and keep the water cool.

- Don't position your pond directly under a tree, or you'll be cleaning out leaves, nuts, and branches constantly.

- Position the pond in an area that won't be contaminated with storm runoff from roofs, lawns, or streams.

- Aquatic plants have benefits and drawbacks. Floating plants such as lilies will keep the pond cool, attract insects, block algae production, and look pretty. However, they can also take over the pond if not kept in check. Submerged plants may make the fish more relaxed and more likely to reproduce, but they can clog the filter.

- Many fish with spines instead of scales are poisonous. Don't stock the pond with fugu (blowfish), barracuda, or piranha—or with water moccasins. Don't use pond fish for sushi.

STEP 9

STEP 10

GROW WHEATGRASS

Wheatgrass has been called "nature's perfect food," though it tastes like, well, lawn trimmings. While some of its more controversial health claims—it prevents hair loss, removes heavy metals from the blood, reduces the side effects of menopause, prevents cancer—remain unproven, wheatgrass is filled with vitamins (especially vitamin B12) and nutrients. Of course, so are most leafy green vegetables. But broccoli and kale aren't easy to grow in your house, and indoor wheatgrass can be harvested less than two weeks after sprouting.

MATERIALS	$10

- ☐ 1–2 cups of wheat berries
- ☐ One metal tray, 2 inches deep, or a seed tray from a garden store
- ☐ Chemical-free potting soil
- ☐ Spray bottle
- ☐ Bowl or jar

- Wheatgrass juice is an acquired taste, somewhere between green tea and weeds. Many people mix it with honey or fruit juices, or just down it quickly like a shot.

- Wheatgrass juice is best served fresh. However, it can be frozen and thawed later. Use an ice cube tray for one-ounce portions.

- Can you use wheatgrass as a replacement for the Bermuda grass on your lawn? Yes. However, winter wheat grows very slowly: It takes about two hundred days to reach its "jointing" stage, when nutrients are at their highest. And it should be hand-cut, not mowed, if you're planning to drink it.

STEPS TO GROW THE WHEATGRASS

1. Soak wheat berries overnight in the bowl or jar. Drain.

2. Spread the soil in the tray to a uniform depth of 1–2 inches.

3. Spread the wheat berries onto the soil so they're touching but not overlapping.

4. Place the tray on a windowsill or other sunny location.

5. Water as needed, using the sprayer. The soil should be moist to the touch at all times. Like most grasses, wheatgrass grows very quickly. It should reach a height of about 7 inches in less than two weeks.

6. Harvest it. Using sharp scissors, cut the grass just above the lower white portion and juice it, using a hand or electric juicer. It can take up to 1 square foot of grass to produce 2 ounces of wheatgrass juice, a typical portion. Note that some people report very high energy levels after drinking just a single 2-ounce serving.

GROW NUT TREES

Like any agricultural pursuit, the cultivation of nut-producing trees depends on many factors, including climate, soil, topography, and insects, to name a few of the bigger ones. But if you're successful, the payoff can be significant. Instead of relying on faraway producers, you'll be growing your own source of protein and "good" fat, potentially cutting your meat consumption, and helping the environment in numerous ways. And as Homer Simpson would say, "Mmmm, nuuuuttttts!"

MATERIALS	$50 (plus ongoing water and fertilization expenses)

- ☐ Sapling
- ☐ Shovel
- ☐ Water
- ☐ Fertilizer, soil, compost, mulch (optional)

Black walnut trees produce a toxin called juglone that is poisonous to many other nearby plants and trees.

STEPS TO GROW THE TREES

1. Choose the proper tree variety. If you're in New York, you shouldn't be planting the same trees as someone who lives in central California (not if you want them to survive, anyway). If you live in the Midwest or Northeast, consider almond, hazelnut, Chinese chestnut, shagbark hickory, some pecan varieties, or black walnut trees (see Green Bits, above, for cautions about black walnuts). In milder climates with a low risk of frost (California, the Southeast) consider almonds, pistachios, pecans, and macadamias.

2. Plant at the proper time. Virtually all saplings will die if planted in late spring or summer, because their root systems aren't established and they cannot survive heat stress. As a rule of thumb, plant in fall or early spring—but only after the risk of frost has passed.

3. Determine spacing. For your tree to produce nuts, you'll typically need a second tree of the same variety, for pollination (check with your nursery). Trees should be no closer than 15 feet apart, and they can be farther if you've got lots of space.

4. Measure the root-ball. The hole you dig for the sapling should be two to three times wider than the root-ball, but only of equal depth.

5. Dig the hole to match your measurements. Many saplings die from drowning: Their roots sit submerged in water, and they succumb to root rot. To keep water off roots, build up a small mound at the center of the hole, surrounded by a trench. Place the tree on the mound. If the roots are wrapped in burlap, cut it away once the tree is in place.

6. Add fertilizer to the bottom of the hole, then fill in the hole with a mixture of soil and compost. (See "Build a Composter," page 164.) The soil-compost mixture should not cover the crown (top) of the tree's root-ball.

7. Water, wait until the soil settles, then backfill. As a general rule, trees require 1 gallon of water for every 6 inches of height. You can use rainwater from a rain barrel.

8. Mulch (optional). Mulch will deter weed growth, add nutrients, and hold moisture. Keep wet mulch away from the tree trunk to prevent rot.

9. Water weekly for the first year.

10. Pick nuts. Depending on the variety, the tree will yield nuts in as little as three years or as long as five to ten years.

- A single healthy tree will release enough oxygen into the atmosphere for two people to breathe for their entire lives.

- The net cooling effect of a young, healthy tree is equivalent to ten room-size air conditioners operating twenty hours a day.

- When properly placed around buildings, trees can reduce air-conditioning needs by 30 percent and can save between 20 and 50 percent in heating energy.

- To estimate your "carbon footprint" and determine how many trees (offsets) you need to plant, visit www.carbonfund.org.

- The U.S. livestock population consumes seven times more grain than Americans do themselves. It takes more than two thousand gallons of water to produce a single pound of beef—not to mention the energy needed to cook all that meat. Nuts are an excellent source of protein and can be eaten raw.

- The United Nations reports that livestock are responsible for 18 percent of greenhouse gas emissions worldwide—more than all the planes, trains, and automobiles on the planet combined.

- A single cow can belch out 130 gallons of methane a day; methane has twenty-one times as much warming potential as CO_2.

- Global meat consumption is expected to more than double by 2050.

NATURAL PEST SOLUTIONS

10 QUICK FIXES

PESTICIDE	PEST	DIRECTIONS FOR USE
Bacillus thuringiensis (Bt)	Caterpillars, hornworms	Spray this naturally occurring bacterium (available at garden stores) directly on plant surfaces and insects; it requires several days to work. Reapply regularly.
Bats	Mosquitoes	Build a bat house (see page 167).
Beer	Slugs	Place small plates of beer in the garden; slugs fall in and drown. Refill after rain.
Boric acid	Ants, roaches, fleas, ticks, millipedes, fungi, molds	Sprinkle boric acid powder (Borax) around the base of plants. Reapply after rain.
Cayenne pepper	Aphids	Mix 1 tablespoon. cayenne powder with 1 quart water, place in a spray bottle, spray on plants. Replace after rain. (It also deters rabbits.)
Cooking oil	Mosquito larvae	Place a few drops of oil into standing water to kill larvae. Replace after rain.
Coyote urine	Deer	Hang urine capsules (available at garden stores) on vegetation and young trees and shrubs; replace as indicated.
French marigolds	Rabbits	Plant amid lettuce and carrots; the strong scent repels rabbits.
Ladybugs	Ants	Scatter them in your garden. (They can be purchased at garden supply stores or online.)
Lavender	Mice, ticks, moths	Plant it in the garden, or place bags of dried lavender on the ground where pests are a problem. Note: Lavender spreads prolifically.

RAISE TROUT IN YOUR SWIMMING POOL

Using a dormant swimming pool as a fish farm is relatively easy and maintenance free, once the water is cleared of chemicals. The fish will also reduce the flying insect population, and they can eventually be eaten. Most home swimming pools are deep enough to allow the fish to overwinter, except in extremely cold climates—where you probably wouldn't have a backyard pool anyway.

MATERIALS	$300 for fingerlings, food pellets, and aerator; not including cost to fill the pool

- ☐ Swimming pool (must be below-grade, and at least 7 feet deep)
- ☐ Fingerlings
- ☐ Pool aerator
- ☐ Food pellets

STEPS TO RAISE THE TROUT

1. Remove all chemicals from the pool. This includes chlorine and any other additives. The pool should contain nothing except freshwater. Because removing all traces of pool chemicals may be difficult, it's best to begin your fish farming when you first fill your pool for the season. Clean and disinfect it first, then rinse well.

2. Adjust the water temperature. Rainbow trout are hardy and excellent eating fish. They prefer colder water but will tolerate temperatures up to about 75°F. If you plan on swimming with the fish and prefer a warmer pool, consider catfish or silver perch, which can survive in temperatures up to a bathwater-like 86°F.

3. Determine your stocking needs. In general, the stocking rates for trout fingerlings (baby trout, 1 to several inches long) are fifty per 1,000 square meters. For an average 20-x-40-foot in-ground swimming pool (800 square feet) you'll need about twelve fish. Don't over-crowd it.

4. Add a water feature. Your trout will die or their growth will be stunted in a stagnant swimming pool. Add a waterfall or some other type of fountain to promote water circulation and aeration.

5. Feed them. Assuming a proper temperature, swimming pool trout will grow at reasonable rates even during the winter, but they'll require frequent feeding, typically once per day. Use commercial food pellets.

6. Catch and cook. Although a typical rainbow trout in the wild will take about four years to reach full size (1 pound), yours may be eaten in about a year, or when they reach "catchable" size, 8–10 inches.

- In the wild, trout spawn in spring. In captivity, they may spawn at any time. However, females bury their eggs in sand and gravel, so unless you plan to convert your pool into a pond—or build one (see page 174)—the fish are unlikely to reproduce.

- A cooler pool will reduce algae blooms.

- Trout can help to reduce a backyard insect problem.

Convert the United States To Solar Energy In Forty Years and Five Easy Steps

OK, so this isn't truly a do-it-yourself, eco-weekend project that can be accomplished with a toolbox and a six-pack of beer. But that's not really the point. Think of this final entry in the book as more of a discussion of what might be, of what could be, if everyone who cares about the future of our environment pushed his or her elected officials to green up our country as you, eco-reader, are going to green up your home.

Three researchers—Ken Zweibel, James Mason, and Vasilis Fthenakis, writing in the January 2008 issue of *Scientific American*—have come up with a "grand plan" to get the United States almost entirely off fossil fuels within forty years. (Al Gore claims it can be done in a decade. But then, he invented the Internet.) Sound crazy? Impossible? Politically, it just may be. But from a technological standpoint, their ideas are exciting and intriguing, and there's nothing inherently pie in the sky about them. The main obstacle? Getting the federal government to contribute a large (though, in relative terms, minuscule) sum of money for the necessary research and infrastructure. After that, the free market takes over. Don't believe it's possible? Read on.

1
PUBLICIZE THE POTENTIAL OF SOLAR POWER

Let's begin with an eye-opening statistic: The energy, in sunlight, striking the earth for forty minutes each day is equivalent to global energy consumption for a *year*. And the United States is sittin' pretty: We have at least 250,000 square miles of land in the Southwest that's suitable for constructing solar power plants. This land receives 4,500 quadrillion British thermal units of solar radiation per year. Converting as little as 2.5 percent of that radiation into electricity would match the nation's current annual energy consumption.

2
CONSTRUCT NEW PV PLANTS

Currently, a measly ten square miles of land are in use in the Southwest, producing 0.5 gigawatts of electricity from solar radiation. The grand plan envisions thirty thousand square miles by 2050, producing 2,940 gigawatts. This sounds like a huge increase, and it is. But studies indicate that the land required to produce each gigawatt-hour of solar energy is actually less than is needed for a coal-powered plant, when factoring in land for coal mining. Of course, coal mining is typically done underground, and solar panels are on the surface. But 80 percent of the land in Arizona is not privately owned. These new plants would displace three hundred coal-fired power plants and their associated emissions.

3
STORE EXCESS SOLAR ENERGY UNDERGROUND

The primary drawback of solar power is obvious: It produces very little electricity when skies are cloudy, and none at night. To address this problem, the plan envisions not battery-based storage, which is common today yet expensive and inefficient, but a system that uses excess electricity to compress air and store it underground—in mines, underground caverns, depleted natural gas wells, and aquifers. The air is released on demand and powers turbines, which generate electricity. (One such plant is already in use in the United States.) The study estimates that 75 percent of the country has such suitable geographic formations, many located near urban areas.

4
BUILD A NEW TRANSMISSION INFRASTRUCTURE

All the electricity created in the Southwest would have to be sent across thousands of miles of transmission wire, in every direction. This is much different from the current generation-and-delivery model, where power plants are relatively close to the areas they serve. The existing alternating current infrastructure is not suitable to carry electricity over vast distances, so a new high-voltage, direct current transmission system would need to be constructed.

5
This is perhaps the most daunting aspect of the plan—though the problem is not insurmountable—and would require government investment. The current economics of solar power are as follows: the efficiency of thin-film modules is 10 percent, the installed cost is $4 per watt, and the electricity price is 16 cents per kilowatt-hour. In order to enable solar power to replace fossil fuels, the researchers have concluded these numbers would have to change to 14 percent efficiency, $1.20 per watt, and 5 cents per kilowatt-hour. More research into materials and improving technological efficiencies is clearly needed. But with government loan guarantees, price support subsidies, and agreements to purchase power, the study says these goals can be met at a cost of about $400 billion over the next forty years. (To be sure, $400 billion is a lot of money, but a little contrast and context is needed here. By some estimates we are spending at least $4 billion in Iraq per *month*.) Over time, the potential savings from moving to solar power are enormous. Unlike traditional power plants, PV plants require little or no fuel to operate, use no water, release no groundwater pollutants, and create zero emissions, saving the country tens of billions of dollars, year after year.

There are other technical hurdles, such as building "concentrated solar" power plants that include heat storage. These plants use special fluids (including molten salt) to retain heat more efficiently. The fluids are then used to produce steam, which drives turbines to create electricity. A few concentrated solar plants exist in the United States today, but none have heat storage; sixteen hours of storage a day would be needed. Other changes—particularly a wholesale shift in the transportation sector to 344 million plug-in hybrid vehicles—might take more time, but they would almost certainly happen if the barriers to market entry and the costs of solar power came down. With the government's price guarantees setting a floor for solar power, at least initially, such barriers would fall quickly.

The potential benefits of eliminating the country's reliance on fossil fuels are compelling. These include massive reductions or eliminations in the importation or local extraction and burning of oil, coal, and natural gas, and a reduction in carbon dioxide emissions from roughly six billion tons today to 2.3 billion in 2050. Millions of new domestic jobs (many in solar panel manufacturing) could be created, and the country's energy use might even fall over time, owing to the elimination of the increasing amounts of energy that would be needed to extract ever-shrinking fossil fuel deposits.

It is indeed a grand plan. Should it happen? Absolutely. Could it happen? Answering that is beyond the scope of this or any book. But one thing's for certain: Change is coming, like it or not. The biggest change—and one that already has a good deal of support in Washington—is likely to be a "carbon tax" on emissions, which means that companies—and particularly energy providers—will no longer be insulated from the environmental costs of their businesses. Yet even small changes to the way we live today, changes like the ones in this book, when magnified millions or billions of times across the globe can have an outsize impact on the planet's ecology.

That noted environmentalist Dick Cheney once scoffed that "conservation may be a sign of personal virtue but it is not a sufficient basis for a sound, comprehensive energy policy." Perhaps not. (Although I'd submit that historically, our energy policy has lacked in everything, including affordable energy.) But we have only one planet—one true home—and conserving energy to make it a better place to live strikes me as very sound policy. And if we can pressure those whose actions (and inaction) affect our planet and its future, through our actions and words and votes, well . . . that's a grand plan well within reach.

ABOUT THE AUTHOR

Josh Piven resides in a windmill, eats nothing that casts a shadow, and takes public transit to work. He is the best-selling author of nineteen books, including the *Worst-Case Scenario Survival Handbook* series and *Bad Vs. Worse*. He has appeared as a survival expert on television around the world. He and his family live—pretty simply—in Philadelphia. (www.joshpiven.net)

ACKNOWLEDGMENTS

Two green thumbs up to everyone at Stewart, Tabori & Chang who believed in this book and helped to make it a reality, especially my editor, Ann Stratton. Special thanks also to my fact-checker Richard Slovak and illustrator Owen Sherwood: You guys rock! (In a very green, very sustainable sort of way . . .)

A

B

C

D

E

F